amy willcock's
aga seasons

amy willcock's
aga seasons

EBURY PRESS
LONDON

DEDICATION

For Janice

First published in Great Britain in 2004

1 3 5 7 9 10 8 6 4 2

Text © Amy Willcock 2004
Photographs © Jason Lowe 2004, except on pages 7, 16–17, 54–55,
106–107, 150–151 and 192 where photographs © Peter Williams 2004

First published by Ebury Press
Random House, 20 Vauxhall Bridge Road, London SW1V 2SA

Random House Australia (Pty) Limited
20 Alfred Street, Milsons Point, Sydney, New South Wales 2061, Australia

Random House New Zealand Limited
18 Poland Road, Glenfield, Auckland 10, New Zealand

Random House South Africa (Pty) Limited
Endulini, 5A Jubilee Road, Parktown 2193, South Africa

The Random House Group Limited Reg. No. 954009

www.randomhouse.co.uk

A CIP catalogue record for this book is available from the British Library.

Editor: Gillian Haslam
Designer: Christine Wood
Photographer: pages 7, 16–17, 54–55, 106–107, 150–151, 192:
Peter Williams; all other photographs: Jason Lowe
Props stylist: pages 3, 117, 127, 129, 135, 137: Pippin Britz; all other
photographs: Tessa Evelegh
Food stylist: pages 3, 117, 127, 129, 135, 137: Anna-Lisa Aldridge;
all other photographs: Sunil Vijayakar

ISBN 0 09 189913 3

Papers used by Ebury Press are natural, recyclable products made from
wood grown in sustainable forests.

Printed and bound in Singapore by Tien Wah

contents

introduction

Liberate your larder, burn your shopping lists and let the seasons decide what you cook tonight!

Forget about tracking down out-of-season produce – not only is it often prohibitively expensive, but the taste can never equal something that has been grown or reared according to its traditional seasonality. All foods – whether fruit or veg, meat or fish – really do taste best when in season and I believe we should support our local markets and farmers as well as the supermarkets. Buy as organically as possible, shun GM foods and basically do the right thing for a healthy lifestyle. Accepting and enjoying the seasons and cooking and eating seasonal dishes will bring back the thrill of anticipation akin to a childhood Christmas.

Enjoying seasonal food is about timing, ripeness, maturity and, ultimately, the cooking, eating and preserving of food as it should be and always was. Seasonality is not just confined to fruit and vegetables, but to everything we consume. When you preserve the harvest, you will know exactly what to do with a glut of fruit and vegetables either from your own garden or the local market.

It would be naive to suggest that in today's world there is a very strict season for everything, so in some cases foods that we eat are available all the year round. Some of these foods are produced in hot houses and I feel they are wholly acceptable, but as a rule try to eat and cook seasonally. As one grower put it, 'nothing is forced, only encouraged'.

I am a great supporter of all things organic so I urge you to start participating in an organic box scheme (see page 11). They are totally governed by the seasons, available throughout the country and the easiest way of going seasonal. I try and buy the best and my philosophy in life is I would rather have a little of the best than a lot of mediocre.

When is a recipe not a recipe?
Certain times of the year, such as late spring and summer, are the times to be led by your senses – you don't need a recipe to be inspired when all you need to do is look at what is

in the markets and shops and do as little to the food as possible. I know it sounds a cliché, but the quality of the ingredients will take you more than half of the way to a great dish. There is a lot of time in the autumn and winter months to cook and stand at the Aga, so enjoy the warmer months and eat raw vegetables with dips and lots of salads and fruits that are in season. Save the winter for tackling new cooking projects.

Something I can't stress strongly enough is that you must develop a feel for food and if something tastes, feels, looks or smells wrong, then change it. There are only a few things that really ruin food – over-salting and burning. Having said that, don't be afraid of salt. I know I will have the 'health police' at my door, but the main difference between home cooking and professional cooking is the seasoning, and by that I mean salt. You also need to understand and be able to see when food is cooked and ready. I know I often use the phrase 'or until it is done', but that is when it is ready and you must be the judge – any cookbook can give you recipes and guidelines, but it is up to the cook to have the basic skills to recognise when the food is ready and at its best. This is essential with all cooking.

I do believe that Aga cookers make people into intuitive cooks because it is easier to grasp these skills with an Aga as your food will not come to any harm when you open the oven doors and have a look. Do cook as much as you can and don't be afraid to make mistakes because that is how you will learn about food. It may be that a course in cooking would help you to become a better cook and give you the skills and confidence to know when food is cooked to perfection. Cooking, essentially, is all about confidence.

Amy Willcock

The Knowledge

This is now my fourth Aga book and my family is convinced that I am officially Aga Gaga! What follows is just a brief guide to Aga cooking methods, so for really in-depth Aga techniques, please read my books *Aga Cooking* and *Amy Willcock's Aga Know-How*.

There is one big rule in Aga cooking:
Keep the lids down and cook in the ovens!

Always remember that 80% of your cooking should be done in the ovens and only 20% on the plates. The Aga cooker's combustion system, heat path and insulation schemes are all designed on this premise. Once you learn to cook like this, you will never suffer heat loss again. I cannot stress this point enough, as it's what the Aga method of cooking is all about.

All the ovens on the right-hand side are externally vented, keeping cooking smells out of the kitchen and succulence in the food. The stored heat is released as radiant heat which is what locks in the flavour and moisture, giving such superb results.

No two Aga cookers are the same. It doesn't matter if they are gas, electric or oil – a burner heats them all in the same way. The heat from the burner unit is transferred to the ovens and hot plates where it is stored. When the insulated lids are down, they hold in the heat. When the lids are up, heat is lost.

Heat lost through cooking is automatically restored. Each Aga is thermostatically controlled, so you can forget about exact temperatures. The mercury in the heat indicator (see above right) should sit on the black line – this means that the Aga has its full amount of stored heat. It is quite usual for the mercury to drop during cooking – don't worry about this as the heat will automatically be restored.

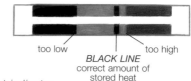

too low   too high
BLACK LINE
correct amount of
stored heat

the heat indicator

There may be times when you are doing a lot of cooking and you feel that you need more heat. Before you start moving the control knob, examine your cooking method – are you using the ovens enough?

As there are no dials to control the temperatures, food is cooked by position and timing. If you think in those terms, adapting conventional recipes will become second nature.

Amy's Golden Rules
1 Keep your lids down!
2 Remember the 80/20 rule. Do the majority of your cooking in the ovens.
3 All the timings and positions given in the recipes are guidelines – no two Aga cookers are alike so you may have to do some moving and adjusting. Always underestimate the timings as dishes can go back in to continue cooking, whereas burnt or ruined food will have to hit the bin.

Equipment
Having the right cookware for an Aga is essential for successful cooking. There is a number of suitable ranges available (please see page 192 for details of stockists and suppliers).

I also love my blowtorch! The truth is that the top of the Aga is not as quick as a grill, so a blowtorch is essential to crisp things up. I use mine all the time, but so do chefs in commercial kitchens so don't feel you are cheating.

Converting Recipes

Converting conventional recipes for Aga use is easy. As all Aga cooking is done by position and timing, just remember how the heat is distributed in each oven and once you decide where the food is to be cooked, adjust the timings accordingly. I usually underestimate the time by about 10 minutes, as I can always put the dish back in for a little longer. Use the recipes in this book as a guide when converting other similar conventional recipes.

Let's take the recipe below – the ingredients and method are exactly the same whether cooking conventionally or in an Aga. The recipe calls for a pre-heated oven, a temperature of 200°C/400°F/gas 6 and a cooking time of 40–45 minutes.

Wild Mushroom and Potato Bake
serves 4

3 tbsp olive oil
250g field and wild mushrooms
1 tbsp chopped fresh rosemary
1 garlic clove, peeled and crushed
salt and pepper
4 large potatoes, peeled and sliced
1 tbsp freshly grated Parmesan cheese

Conventional instructions:
Pre-heat the oven to 200°C/400°F/gas 6. Heat 1 tablespoon of the oil in a frying pan and gently fry the mushrooms until lightly coloured. Add the rosemary, garlic, salt and pepper and cook for about 1 minute, then set aside. Layer half the sliced potatoes into a dish, put half the mushrooms on top and repeat. Drizzle over the remaining olive oil and sprinkle with cheese. Bake for 40 minutes until bubbling and golden on top.

To convert for the Aga:
First, there's no need to pre-heat the oven as the Aga is always ready to cook. Start off by heating the pan and oil on the Roasting Oven floor, add the mushrooms and cook until coloured. Then move the pan to the Simmering Plate and cook the garlic and herbs until the garlic is softened. Continue as before with layering the potatoes, then put the dish into the lower/bottom half of the Roasting Oven on the third or fourth set of runners. Estimate the time at 40 minutes, but it may take up to an hour if you have been cooking a lot and the oven is not right up to temperature, or less time if the oven is really hot. Have a look at it throughout the cooking time and check for doneness at about 25 minutes. If browning too quickly on top, cover with foil or the Cold Plain Shelf.

Seasonal Entertaining

Nothing drives me madder than when I go to someone's house for dinner and they serve asparagus in mid winter. Please note this if I ever come round for dinner! Try to plan your menu and your cooking around the season and your Aga.

Consider logistics. Invariably food moves around the Aga, usually ending up in the Warming or Simmering Ovens, on the Warming Plate or on protected hot plate lids. Plan to use the space they leave in the ovens well. You may find that you cook food in a different order than usual as the safety net of the Simmering or Warming Ovens allows for greater flexibility.

First, write a timetable (a sort of meal countdown) when cooking for entertaining or large parties.
- Decide the menu according to season and what's available in the market, garden or supermarket.
- Plan in which order to cook the recipes according to oven space and the heat required.
- Decide which recipes can be cooked ahead and take into account thawing times and re-heating times if applicable. It is always advisable to plan on serving some foods that can be completely done ahead and just need re-heating.

- Try out new recipes before the big occasion. As well as averting disaster, you will be able to judge holding times for the Simmering or Warming Ovens.

To help you plan your entertaining, I have worked out a menu timetable using two of the recipes in this book. It is simply a guideline so please improvise and change it to suit your own menu. My recipe books are full of scribbled notes on the sides of recipes to help me with cooking times or positions of tins. I have omitted freezing and thawing, only to give you even more flexibility if you wish. I have also assumed that you can do the preparation the day before.

You will also notice that here I have used the slow roasting method which I use all the time for lamb and pork, but roast rib of beef is always cooked in the conventional way. Using conventional cooking methods for lamb and pork is absolutely fine but you will have more flexibility when using the slow method. Meats done this way will be tender and juicy and will be medium to well done. For rare lamb use the conventional roasting method.

Weekend Spring Lunch Menu

Lamb in a Hay Box (page 30)
Boiled New Potatoes
Purple Sprouting Broccoli
Panna Cotta with Baked Rhubarb (page 50)

The Day Before:
- Blanch the purple sprouting broccoli and transfer to a heatproof serving dish. Drizzle over some olive oil, cover with foil and put them into the fridge. (Or you can just cook on the day.)
- Make the panna cotta and baked rhubarb, or make them early the next day. Wrap in clingfilm and put into the fridge.

Day of Lunch:
Early in the morning:
- Prepare the leg of lamb (see page 30).

9:30am:
- Put the lamb into the Roasting Oven for 1½ hours.
- Put gravy boats, plates and serving dishes in the Simmering Oven or Warming Oven and on top of the Aga to warm.

11:00am:
- Transfer the lamb to the Simmering Oven.

12:00pm:
- Bring the new potatoes to the boil on the Boiling Plate, then drain off the water, add a knob of butter and season. Cover with a lid and cook in the Simmering Oven.

12:45pm:
- Take the prepared broccoli out of the fridge and bring to room temperature.

1:15pm:
- Put the broccoli into the Roasting Oven to re-heat for about 10 minutes.
- Take the lamb out of the oven and rest. Pour the pan juices into gravy boats and keep warm.
- Transfer the potatoes to serving dishes.

1:30pm:
- Carve the lamb and enjoy lunch.

Remove the panna cotta from the fridge when you clear the plates, to allow it to soften. If you want to serve a hot pudding like crumble, make it and cook it first thing in the morning, then put it and the pudding plates into the Simmering Oven to heat up just before you sit down to lunch.

Seasonal Produce

To help you decide what to cook when, at the beginning of each chapter there is a list of the foods in season for the relevant months. I have listed foods when they are usually at their best, but of course weather patterns, such as late frosts or an early summer, can affect this. Throughout the country, some varieties of produce appear earlier or later than others, so use these lists as a general guide but take notice of what's growing in your own garden or what is available in markets and farm shops.

While writing this book I have had a little voice inside my head saying, 'Yes, all this seasonal stuff is great, but what about lemons? What about lettuces? What about all those other fruits and vegetables we use all year round?' The only thing I can say is, hand on heart, I do buy lemons and other produce all year round. I buy organic as much as possible and, yes, I do buy things that are out of season. I console myself with the fact that they are grown organically in polytunnels by my local organic farm or grown and imported by reputable organic growers. As long as people buy UK produce when it's in season, I don't have a problem with people buying imported food when there is no other option. However, my aim with this book is to demonstrate the huge variety of fresh, seasonal produce that is available to us throughout the year and to revive interest in the sometimes forgotten fruits and vegetables.

Buying Organic

One of the best ways to cook and eat seasonally is to join an organic box scheme. A local organic supplier delivers a box of produce to you each week, the contents varying according to what is in season. Some box schemes supply just fruit and veg, while others can also deliver meat and fish. If you are interested in joining an organic box scheme, contact The Soil Association (see page 192).

The whole point of organic production – whether it's for meat and dairy, or fruit and veg – goes deeper than simply avoiding the use of pesticides and fertilisers. It is about working with nature rather than trying to control it, emphasising soil and land management, and encouraging good animal husbandry to enhance and protect the land. Non-farmed land is just as important as farmed. Crop rotation and good husbandry to manage soil, fertility, pest, disease and weed control are the main aspects of organic farming.

Any item of food can legally only be labelled organic when its production – from sowing, or birth, to your table – has been monitored and passed the strict criteria laid down by an approved government body. This is your guarantee as a consumer that you are getting what you have asked and paid for. The use of any form of genetically modified organisms is strictly prohibited in the production of organic food worldwide.

Choosing Fruit and Vegetables

Don't waste time or money using inferior produce. Ripeness is something you need to be able to decipher at the market stall. To determine if something is ripe, or near to it, or indeed at the stage of ripeness you want it (such as green tomatoes), you need to use your senses – touch it, smell it, look at it and if possible taste it! You need to do this every time you buy something. You won't always get it right because food is a living object but practise will make you a better judge. Do not settle for anything less than the best. You only have to go to a continental market to see the discerning buyers – follow their lead.

Herbs

Herbs are easy to grow and to buy in pots from the supermarket, so there is no excuse for not using fresh herbs! If you do grow them yourself, try to site your herb garden near your kitchen door and try to follow the organic way of growing by companion planting throughout your garden – it will help your plants and your cooking.

I don't really like using dried herbs much. I do have some as back-up for the winter months, although I do cheat and buy fresh herbs grown in polytunnels throughout the year. If you have fresh herbs and eggs, you always have a winning supper in your kitchen – the perfect herb omelette!

Nuts

I love nuts of all sorts but especially wet walnuts (sometimes called green walnuts) and fresh-from-the-tree hazelnuts (also called filberts). When these are in season, I pile them into a small old wooden trug and serve them with cheese. The freshness is surprising to those who haven't tried them before.

When you are using nuts in a recipe, if time allows do grind your own nuts (such as almonds and walnuts) as it does make a difference to the final taste – but don't worry if you need to use the pre-chopped or ground ones bought in bags. The perfect tool is a microplane rotary grater. I buy organic nuts and always roast them before using. Watch them like a hawk or they will burn.

Of course freshness is the key to most things, but I must admit I do like a bit of vacuum packing! Fresh chestnuts are wonderful roasted fireside or indeed in an Aga, but when time is my enemy I do resort to the vac-packed ones.

The Dairy

Traditionally spring, especially the month of May, was a very busy time for dairymaids with cattle returned to their spring pastures. The dairy farmer was able to milk his herd three times a day, making this the time to preserve milk by turning it into cheese and butter.

Cheeses made with spring and summer milk are generally considered the best and are ready for eating at Christmas time. This, of course, is purely a matter of taste as some people prefer cheeses made in the winter months with milk from cows fed on a more cereal-based diet.

With falling milk prices, many dairy farmers have had to diversify to cheese making to help supplement the farm income. Cattle are bred to suit the farmer and nowadays there really isn't a season for cheeses or beef as modern farming methods mean dairy products can be made all year round. Some goat's cheeses and some French cheeses, such as Vacherin Mont d'Or, are seasonal so the trick is to go to a good cheesemonger and try out new and interesting cheeses and ask for information on the regions, characteristics and seasons of the cheese.

A British cheese which used to be seasonal is Cheddar. Cheddar is made from milk in the late summer and it accounts for more than half of all cheese sales in the UK, with a growing trend for stronger tasting cheeses matured for 9, 12 or 15 months. When holidaying in the UK, it is well worth going to the local tourist offices as most can provide information on the local cheese producers. Another great place to find out information about cheese is The British Cheese website www.britishcheese.com, or visit www.demelle.com, which is linked to the well-known London cheese shop La Fromagerie (see page 192).

Storing Cheese

To get the very best out of your cheeses, store them properly as they will taste better and your enjoyment will last longer.

- Hard cheese: wrap the cheese in clean cling film, leaving the crust or rind unwrapped. Do not reuse the old cling film to re-wrap the cheese – always tear off a new piece.
- Soft cheeses and blue cheeses: ideally, first wrap them in old-fashioned waxed paper. This can be hard to track down (see page 192), so alternatively wrap in greaseproof paper, then in foil.
- Goat's cheese: store this on a plate with an upturned bowl as a cover. A cake tin also works well – put the cheese on the lid and invert the deep tin over the top.

Never store cheese unwrapped with other foods as the flavour or smell of one may taint the other. As well as storing cheese in the fridge, I also use a cheese safe – it has tile shelves for coolness and mesh sides for air circulation. If you're lucky enough to have one, an old-fashioned cool larder is also excellent.

The Larder

To cook well and put a meal together quickly and easily, you need to keep a well-stocked larder or pantry. Testing new recipes will be less daunting if all the basics are at hand and only a few special ingredients need to be bought. I include the freezer as part of my overall larder – my children love to help me to make pastry and on rainy days we often stock up the freezer with sweet and savoury pastry dough, which means that creating a fabulous pudding or starter is as easy as pie!

Here is a list of what I call my basic larder. Don't be put off by the length of it – you will probably already have many of the items listed.

Dry store

Mustard:
English mustard powder
Dijon

Vinegar:
Balsamic
Red wine
White wine

Oil:
Grapeseed
Olive oil (mild and
  extra virgin)
Sunflower
Walnut

Spices:
Cardamom pods
Cayenne pepper
Cinnamon
Coriander seeds
Crushed chillies
Cumin
Fennel seeds
Juniper berries
Madras curry powder
Saffron
Smoked paprika
Whole cloves
Whole nutmegs, with
  mace casing intact
Whole vanilla pods
I do also keep a few
  dried herbs, but I
  mainly use fresh.

Flour:
'00' pasta flour
Cornflour
Plain flour
Potato flour
Rice flour (essential for
  people with a wheat
  intolerance)
Self-raising flour
Strong bread flour

Dried pasta:
Macaroni
Spaghetti
Tagliatelle
plus any other shapes
  you like to use

Rice:
Arborio
Basmati
Jasmine
Pudding rice

Sugar (unrefined):
Demerara sugar
Golden caster sugar
Granulated sugar
Icing sugar
Vanilla sugar (home made)

Bottled sauces:
Concentrated liquid
  chicken stock
Organic tomato ketchup
Soy sauce

Tabasco
Tomato paste
Worcestershire sauce

Tinned goods:
Anchovies in olive oil
Borlotti beans
Chickpeas
Kidney beans
Lentils
Plum tomatoes
Sun-dried tomatoes
Sweetcorn
Tuna in olive oil

Nuts:
Almonds (chopped,
  flaked and ground)
Hazelnuts
Pecans
Pine nuts
Walnuts

Preserves:
Apricot jam
Golden syrup
Honey
Marmalade
Mint in golden syrup
Redcurrant jelly
Strawberry jam

Dried fruits:
Apricots
Dates
Figs

Raisins
Sour cherries
Sultanas

Good-quality dark
  chocolate (at least
  70% cocoa solids)

In the freezer
Bacon
Butter
Chicken breasts
Gold-top milk
Petits pois
Sausages
Sweet and savoury
  pastry dough in tart tins

In the refrigerator
Bacon
Butter
Cheddar cheese
Crème fraîche
Double cream
Dripping
Eggs
Milk
Natural yoghurt
Pancetta
Parmesan cheese

In the fruit bowl
Apples
Bananas
Grapes
Organic lemons

Preserving the Harvest

There are a number of ways in which to preserve the harvest. Fruit and vegetables can be preserved using simple methods, while animal foods need to be cured and are more complicated. Nothing gives the home cook more satisfaction than seeing the shelves of the larder groaning with jars of home-made jam and preserved fruit. Of course, the easiest method of preserving is freezing, but some foods (such as courgettes, broad beans and strawberries) can suffer from loss of taste.

Three types of organisms cause deterioration in home-preserved fruit and vegetables – yeasts, moulds and bacteria. Yeasts and moulds grow in fruit in the presence of acid, which is why only perfect fruit should be used. If the fruit is bruised or broken, yeasts and moulds from the atmosphere attack the fruit. Vegetables have no acid, so yeasts and moulds have no effect upon them. They are, however, attacked by earth bacteria which are more difficult for the home cook to destroy than yeasts and moulds. It is for this food safety reason that I do not recommend bottling vegetables. In fact, all home bottling is not recommended and it should only be done in a commercially approved environment.

When preserving, bear in mind the following:

● Yeasts and moulds do not like extreme or prolonged heat, excess sugar or the exclusion of air and moisture. Bacteria do not like clean surroundings, heat, acid or harmless antiseptics.

● Always use heat-safe glass bottles and jars with wide necks and new rubber seals or tight fitting lids. (Rubber seals can only be used once.) Do not use cracked or chipped jars or bottles as they could harbour bacteria.

● Fruit with large stones must have them removed otherwise a small amount of prussic acid from the stones will give the fruit a bitter taste.

● Use a stainless steel knife to cut the fruit as it will not cause fruit to discolour.

Jams and Chutneys

There are times of the year, mainly late summer and early autumn, when we can be inundated with gluts of fruit and veg. This is the time to make all your jams and chutneys. Making berry-based jams in the oven intensifies the flavour of the fruit and is really easy (see page 148).

Chutneys are the easiest way to preserve the harvest (see pages 96–99 for recipes). They are always a mixture of sweet and sour, halfway between a pickle and a jam. You can let your garden harvest dictate the base and let your imagination (and spice cupboard) run wild. Fruit should be chopped so that it is small enough to fit on to a teaspoon but not so small that it turns to mush. I believe all chutneys taste better with age so I restrain myself from using them for about a month. Serve them with cold meats and cheeses, and they are a fabulous way to add that something extra to casseroles and curries.

There are a few golden rules when preserving:

● Make jams, jellies and marmalades when your Aga is at its hottest, such as first thing in the morning.

● Use dry, unblemished fruit.

● All equipment must be scrupulously clean.

● All jars and lids must be sterilised. If you have a dishwasher, put them through a high heat cycle, or sterilise with boiling water, then place on a baking tray and slide them into the Simmering Oven for 10–15 minutes. Keep them warm when you pour in the jam. Always seal jars while the contents are hot.

● Warm sugar and fruits in the Simmering or Warming Oven before using.

● If a recipe calls for a fruit that needs to be cooked before adding the sugar, use as little water as possible and cover the pan with a tight fitting lid. Bring to the boil on the Boiling Plate, then transfer to the Simmering Oven until it is ready.

● Skim scum frequently when the jam is boiling and add a small knob of butter to disperse it at the end of the cooking time.

- To test for a good set, put a few saucers into a freezer before you begin. After the first 20 minutes or so of rapid boiling, take a saucer from the freezer and drop a small spoonful of the jam on to the cold saucer. Allow it to cool for a minute, then push your finger through the jam. If it wrinkles it is ready, if not, boil for a few more minutes. Carry on testing until a set has been reached. Always remove the jam from the heat when you are testing so that if it is ready, you will not overcook it.

Drying Foods

This is where the 4-oven Aga really comes into its own, although it is just as easy with a 2-oven Aga.

Slice the fruit or vegetables into 1–2cm slices or into halves or quarters. Lay on a shallow baking tray lined with a piece of Bake-O-Glide. Slide the tray into the Warming Oven in a 4-oven Aga for 6–8 hours or leave overnight. The juicier the fruit, the longer it will take to dry out. It is best to scoop out the fleshy insides of things like tomatoes before slicing. In a 2-oven Aga slide the tray on to the third set of runners in the Simmering Oven for 3–6 hours. If I don't need my Aga for anything else, I sometimes leave the door ajar. Store the dried vegetables or fruit in jars with tight fitting lids and rehydrate with boiling water when required.

Leave mushrooms whole and start them off in the Simmering or Warming Ovens, then transfer to the lid of the Boiling Plate, protected by a tea towel until they are really dry. Store in an airtight bag or jar and re-hydrate with boiling water.

At Christmas, dry out orange and pear slices until they are really stiff and hard. Spray with hairspray, then thread a ribbon through them and hang on the Christmas tree or use for decorating wreaths and flower arrangements.

Drying herbs couldn't be simpler – take a bunch of whatever you want to dry out and tie together really tightly as they will shrink when dried, then hang them over the Aga. Store in jars.

Sicilian lemon relish (page 100)

spring

what's in season?

March

Fruit
Forced rhubarb

Vegetables
Brussels sprouts
Cabbage (Savoy)
Carrots (stored)
Cauliflower
Celeriac
Garlic (new and
  stored)
Leeks
Nettles
Onions (new and
  stored)
Parsnips
Potatoes (main crop
  and stored, see
  note on page 179)
Purple sprouting
  broccoli
Rocket (in
  polytunnels)
Shallots (new and
  stored)
Spinach
Spring greens
Swedes
Tomatoes (hot
  house)
Watercress

Herbs
Chives
Rosemary

Sage
Thyme

Meat
Guinea fowl
Hare
Pigeon
Pork
Quail
Rabbit
Venison

Fish and seafood
John Dory
Monkfish
Oysters
Sea bass
Wild salmon

Dairy
Cheese (fresh
  goat's cheese)

April

Fruit
Rhubarb (forced
  and outdoor)

Vegetables
Cabbage
Cauliflower
Garlic (stored)
Hop shoots
Leeks
Lettuce (in
  polytunnels)

Morel mushrooms
Nettles
Onions (stored)
Potatoes (stored)
Purple sprouting
  broccoli
Radishes
Shallots (stored)
Sorrel
Spinach
Spring greens
Wild garlic
Wild rocket
Watercress

Herbs
Chives
Mint
Rosemary
Thyme

Fish and seafood
Crab
Sea trout
Wild salmon

Dairy
Fresh cheeses (curd,
  goat's, ricotta)

May

Fruit
Outdoor rhubarb

Vegetables
Asparagus

Garlic (stored)
Hop shoots
Lettuce
Morel mushrooms
Onions (stored)
Potatoes (stored)
Radishes
Rocket
Shallots (stored)
Sorrel
Spring greens
Watercress
Wild garlic

Herbs
Chives
Elderflowers
Mint
Rosemary
Sage
Thyme

Meat
Chicken
Milk-fed lamb

Fish and seafood
Sea trout
Spider crab
Wild salmon

Dairy
Butter
Eggs (natural egg
  laying time)
Soft cheeses
Yoghurt

spring recipes

Soups and Starters

Ramsom and Nettle Soup

Smoked Salmon Pâté

Parma Ham and Asparagus Wraps

Baked Egg Croustades with Black Pudding
and Bacon

Asparagus with Fried Eggs and Savoury
Breadcrumbs

Main Courses/Meat

Spring Chicken

Asian Chicken

Lime and Cardamom Chicken

Easter Turkey

Wild Rice Stuffing

Rack of Veal with Spring Looko

Wiener Schnitzel

Lamb in a Hay Box

Milk-fed Lamb with Lavender

Main Courses/Fish and Seafood

Langoustines with Garlic and Tarragon

Lemon and Lime Fish Cakes

Roasted Salmon with Sorrel and Capers

Trout with Fennel

Little Brown Trout with Hazelnuts

Fish Dusting Powder

Main Courses/Vegetarian

Roasted Asparagus with Dippy Eggs
and Parmesan

Roasted Vegetables in Batter

Baked Egg with Potted Shrimps

Classic Baked Eggs

Potato Gnocchi

Spring Pizza

Accompaniments

Spinach with Pine Nuts and Raisins

Pickled White Cabbage

Creamed Spinach

Purple Sprouting Broccoli with Potted
Shrimps

Roasted Cauliflower with Pancetta
and Taleggio

Baby Carrots glazed with Balsamic Butter

Desserts and Baking

Crème Brûlée

Milk and Honey Jelly

Panna Cotta

Baked Rhubarb

Baked Ricotta Cheesecake

Fairy Cakes

Ramsoms are wild garlic. You may see them growing by the roadside in early spring. Where I live on the Isle of Wight, we have loads of them and I have some in my garden – if you do grow them, be careful as they spread like wild fire! Nettles make wonderful soup and they are free – all you have to do is protect your hands with rubber gloves while preparing them.

ramsom and nettle soup

serves 4

olive oil

1 large onion, peeled and chopped

2 potatoes, peeled and chopped into small cubes

2 handfuls of nettle heads, wash with gloved hands and trim away the stems

4–6 ramsom leaves, washed

1 litre chicken or vegetable stock

salt and pepper

150ml cream

1 Heat up some oil in a deep pan on the Simmering Plate. Soften the onion in the oil, then add the potatoes, nettles and ramsom leaves. Pour in the chicken stock.

2 Bring up to the boil, then cover and transfer to the Simmering Oven. Cook for 30–40 minutes or until the potatoes are soft. Liquidise the soup in a food processor or with an electric hand blender.

3 Season with salt and pepper and return to the Simmering Plate for a few minutes. Stir in the cream and serve with soda bread (see page 113).

Conventional Cooking:
Make on the hob.

smoked salmon pâté

serves 6–8

400g smoked salmon, chopped into pieces

100g soft unsalted butter

pepper

140g fromage frais or cream cheese

4 tbsp double cream or crème fraîche

1 tbsp chopped fresh dill

zest of ½ small organic lemon, plus juice to taste

clarified butter (see page 118)

1 Put the salmon, unsalted butter, pepper, fromage frais or cream cheese, double cream or crème fraîche, dill and lemon zest into the bowl of a food processor and blitz until smooth. Check the consistency – you want a smooth pâté, nothing too loose or too stiff (if it is too stiff add a bit more double cream). Check the seasoning. I like to add lemon juice to taste – this is optional.

2 Tip the pâté into a dish and cover with melted clarified butter. Serve with lemon wedges and toast.

Note:
You can actually use any smoked fish in this recipe. If you use fromage frais, use the double cream; if you use cream cheese, use the crème fraîche.

I never tire of asparagus because its season is so short but I abhor eating it out of season. The first harvest of asparagus always gets the classic hollandaise treatment in our house. When you are preparing asparagus, snap it between your fingers to remove the woody stems, then trim them with a knife. The asparagus will naturally snap at the softest point, leaving you only the tender bits (use the ends for soup). If you are using later asparagus, you may wish to peel the stem to remove all traces of toughness.

parma ham and asparagus wraps

serves 6–8

24 thick asparagus spears, trimmed

24 slices Parma ham

24 thin slices Gruyère cheese

8 soft-boiled eggs, peeled and chopped

25g butter, plus more for greasing dish and topping

100g flour

500ml milk

250g Gruyère cheese, grated

salt and pepper

handful of breadcrumbs (made from stale focaccia or ciabatta bread, or store-bought ciabatta crispbreads)

1 Cook the asparagus spears in a pan of boiling water on the Boiling Plate for 2 minutes and drain. Plunge into iced water and drain again.

2 Lay out a slice of ham with a slice of cheese on top, then place an asparagus spear on it and roll up so that you have an asparagus spear wrapped in the cheese and ham. Continue until they are all used up.

3 Butter an ovenproof dish and lay the rolls in the dish, as flat as possible but this will depend on the size of your dish. Scatter over the chopped egg.

4 Make the sauce. Melt the butter in a non-stick saucepan on the Simmering Plate, add the flour and cook for 2–3 minutes. Add the milk little by little, stirring all the time, until it is all used and you have a luscious white sauce. Remove the pan from the heat, add half of the grated cheese and season.

5 Pour the sauce over the asparagus rolls, then sprinkle over the rest of the cheese and the breadcrumbs. Bake on the third set of runners in the Roasting Oven for 20–25 minutes or until golden and bubbling. Serve with lots of crusty bread and a salad.

Conventional Cooking:

Make the sauce on the hob. Pre-heat the oven to 180°C/350°F/gas 4 and cook as above.

Note:

You can also make an equally delicious winter version of this dish using leeks rather than asparagus.

baked egg croustades with black pudding and bacon

serves 6

6 slices thinly sliced organic bread, crusts removed

3–4 tbsp melted butter or olive oil

4 rashers bacon, cooked and chopped

6 slices black pudding (this normally does not need to be cooked first, but check the instructions on the packet)

double cream

pepper

6 small or medium eggs

1 To make the croustades, using a rolling pin, roll out each slice of bread and brush with the butter or oil. Press one slice of bread into each slot of a muffin tin. Bake in the Roasting Oven or Baking Oven for 5–8 minutes or until just beginning to turn brown. Remove from the oven.

2 Fill each croustade with some chopped bacon, a slice of black pudding, a dribble of cream and some pepper, then crack an egg on top. Put back in the Roasting Oven and bake until the eggs are just set and a bit runny.

Conventional Cooking:

Pre-heat the oven to 180°C/350°F/gas 4 and bake as above.

Note:

Croustades are so versatile that you can fill them with almost anything – hot or cold. They can be made a day in advance or frozen for up to two weeks.

asparagus with fried eggs and savoury breadcrumbs

stale peasant bread

olive oil

shallots, peeled and finely chopped

finely chopped fresh herbs (such as parsley or tarragon)

salt and pepper

asparagus

eggs

smoked salmon (optional)

red wine vinegar

1 Take some good, stale peasant bread and whiz into breadcrumbs (make sure they are not uniform – you want some chunky and some fine).

2 Heat some olive oil in a frying pan on the Simmering Plate and brown the shallots. Add the breadcrumbs and cook until golden and crispy, then add the herbs and salt and pepper. Toss around the frying pan. Drain the bread-crumbs on kitchen paper and set aside. Wipe the frying pan but don't wash it.

3 Steam or boil the asparagus, drain and keep warm. Add more olive oil to the frying pan and fry your eggs – one per person. Arrange the asparagus spears on the plate(s), add a slice of smoked salmon if you like, pop the egg on top of the smoked salmon and scatter over the breadcrumbs.

4 Deglaze the frying pan with some red wine vinegar and spoon the liquid over the egg and asparagus. Season with salt and pepper and enjoy.

Conventional Cooking:

Cook on the hob.

Note:

I write this recipe more as a general method than giving precise amounts and timings. Choose the quantities according to how many you are feeding.

baked egg croustades with black pudding and bacon

MAIN COURSES/MEAT

spring chicken

serves 4

olive oil

1kg chicken thighs, fat and skin removed

butter

1 onion, peeled and finely chopped

6–8 large asparagus spears (second grade), cut into 4cm pieces

600ml chicken stock

salt and pepper

300g puntaletta or orzo (rice shaped pasta)

small handful chopped fresh flat leaf parsley

large handful watercress leaves, chopped

1 Heat up some olive oil in a large casserole on the Simmering or Boiling Plate or on the floor of the Roasting Oven and brown all the chicken pieces in batches. Remove to a dish. Drain off the fat and add a little butter and fry the onion until it is soft.

2 Put the chicken back into the casserole and add the asparagus, stock, salt and pepper. Bring up to the boil on the Boiling Plate and stir well. Cover the casserole with a lid and transfer it to the Roasting Oven for 25 minutes, then add the puntaletta and continue to cook for another 10–12 minutes or until the pasta is al dente. Feel free to add more stock or water if it looks like it needs it.

3 Remove from the oven and stir in the watercress and flat leaf parsley. Serve in bowls with crusty bread.

Conventional Cooking:

Brown the meat on the hob, then pre-heat the oven to 200°C/400°F/gas 6 and cook as above.

asian chicken

serves 6

300ml soy sauce

300ml sweet Indonesian soy sauce (also called kecap manis)

300ml chicken stock

120ml honey

60g brown sugar

1 whole star anise

1 tsp Chinese 5-spice powder

6 whole spring onions, trimmed and tied into knots

45ml sherry

3 garlic cloves, peeled

4cm piece of ginger, grated

3kg organic free-range chicken

1 Put all of the ingredients except the chicken into a large casserole with a lid and bring to the boil on the Boiling Plate. Stir until the sugar has dissolved. Add the chicken to the pot, breast side down, and bring back to the boil.

2 Transfer the casserole to the fourth set of runners in the Roasting Oven for 1 hour, then turn the chicken over and move to the Simmering Oven for another 1–1½ hours.

3 Remove the casserole from the oven, transfer the chicken to a warmed platter and cover. Rest for 15 minutes.

4 While the chicken is resting, bring the sauce back to the boil on the Boiling Plate until it is thick and syrupy. When you are ready to serve, spoon over some of the sauce and serve with wedges of lime.

Conventional Cooking:

Pre-heat the oven to 180°C/350°F/gas 4 and cook the chicken as above.

Note:

This dish is also great cold. To serve cold, remove the casserole from the oven and let the chicken cool in the cooking liqueur for about 2 hours. You can also use duck, but there will be more fat so drain away all the excess.

lime and cardamom chicken

serves 6

3cm piece fresh ginger, peeled

2 garlic cloves, peeled

seeds from 2 tsp cardamom (crush them in a mortar and pestle and remove seeds)

small bunch of coriander, plus extra to serve

juice and zest of 2 organic limes

salt and pepper

6 chicken breasts, bone in

500ml Greek yoghurt, drained

1 tsp cornflour

clarified butter (see page 118)

400ml tin coconut milk

1 green chilli, or more if you like it really hot, chopped

1 Put the ginger, garlic, cardamom seeds and coriander into a food processor and make into a paste. Grate the zest of the limes and add them to the paste. Season with salt and pepper and stir well.

2 Smear the chicken breasts with the paste and leave in a plastic bag or bowl covered with cling film overnight in the fridge. Remove from the fridge 20 minutes before you want to cook them.

3 Mix the yoghurt with the cornflour. Heat about a tablespoon of clarified butter in a large pan on the Boiling Plate or on the floor of the Roasting Oven until it is really hot. Gently brown the chicken, then transfer to a plate.

4 Add the rest of the paste left in the bag or bowl to the pan and fry for a minute. Add the coconut milk to deglaze the pan, stir well, then add the yoghurt/cornflour mix (add a little water if it becomes too thick).

5 Return the chicken to the pan and add the chilli. Stir well, cover and bring to a rapid simmer on the Simmering Plate, then move to the Simmering Oven and cook for 30–35 minutes or until the chicken is cooked. Check the seasoning and squeeze over the lime juice. Serve with rice and lime wedges and more freshly chopped coriander.

Conventional Cooking:
Brown the meat on the hob, then continue as above in an oven pre-heated to 190°C/375°F/gas 5.

easter turkey

By the time Easter comes round it is so long since Christmas that everyone will be enthusiastic about eating turkey again! It is great for feeding crowds and my advice is to roast the turkey in the usual way, basting it with clarified butter (see page 118) every hour or so. For an Easter turkey, try serving it with Wild Rice Stuffing (see below right) and Waldorf salad as a change from the usual trimmings.

   The Aga can accommodate a turkey up to 12.5kg and I recommend investing in a turkey roasting tin. There are two methods of roasting turkey: the slow roasting method, which can be left overnight, and the conventional method. The advantage of the slow method is that you don't have to worry about the turkey and the Roasting Oven will be free to cook all the traditional trimmings. Timings are approximate and very much depend on the size of the bird. The timings may have to be increased for older Aga cookers if you use the slow method.

Preparing a fresh turkey

Wash the turkey with water and pat dry with kitchen towel. Stuff only the neck end of the bird and put a couple of onions into the body cavity. Season well with salt and pepper. Put the turkey into the roasting tin. Do not truss the bird. Generously brush melted clarified butter all over the bird. The secret to a succulent golden bird is in the basting. Leave the pot of clarified butter at the back of the Aga so that it is within easy reach for frequent basting (about every 30 minutes during cooking). It is now ready for the oven.

Slow roasting method

Place the roasting tin directly on to the floor of the Roasting Oven and cook for about 1 hour or until the turkey is browned. A larger turkey may take longer to brown. It is essential to give the turkey a real blast of heat for a good amount of time for food safety. When it is browned, baste with the clarified butter, cover loosely with foil and move to the Simmering Oven for the following time:

3.6–4.5kg: 3–6 hours
4.5–7.25kg: 5–8½ hours
7.25–9kg: 8½–11 hours
9–11kg: 11–13½ hours
11–12.5kg: 13½–15½ hours
All times are approximate.

*Conventional or
fast roasting method*

Place the roasting tin on the floor of the Roasting Oven. After about 1 hour, or when the turkey is browned, cover loosely with foil and cook for the following times:

3.6–4.5kg: 1½–2 hours
4.5 7.25kg: 2–2½ hours
7.25 9kg: 2½–3 hours
9–11kg: 3½–4½hours
11–12.5kg: 4½–5½ hours
All times are approximate.

The turkey is done when the thigh juices run clear when pierced with a skewer or use a meat thermometer.

Rest the turkey for at least 20 minutes. A large bird will stay hot for a long time and can withstand a long time resting. Take this into consideration when working out your cooking timetable.

wild rice stuffing

serves 6

250g wild rice
2 tbsp olive oil
1 large red onion, peeled and chopped
80g sultanas
125g Parmesan cheese
1 heaped tbsp chopped fresh chives
1 heaped tbsp chopped fresh flat leaf parsley
2 tbsp balsamic vinegar
salt and pepper
butter, for greasing

1 Put the rice in a large pan of water and bring to the boil on the Boiling Plate. Stir once, then cover with a lid and place on the floor of the Simmering Oven for 18–20 minutes or until tender but still with a bite.
2 While the rice is cooking, heat the olive oil in a pan on the floor of the Roasting Oven, add the onion and cook until soft and translucent. Set aside.
3 When the rice is ready, tip it into a large bowl. Stir in all the remaining ingredients, except the butter but including the cooked onions. Butter an ovenproof dish, put the stuffing in and cover with foil.
4 Bake on the third set of runners in the Roasting Oven for 20 minutes.

Conventional Cooking:
Cook the rice and the onions on the hob. Pre-heat the oven to 200°C/400°F/gas 6 and cook the stuffing for 25 minutes.

rack of veal with spring leeks

serves 6

4 shallots, peeled

1 garlic clove, peeled

2 tbsp fresh rosemary

2 tbsp fresh thyme

3 tbsp butter

salt and pepper

3 tbsp freshly grated Parmesan cheese

6 tbsp fresh breadcrumbs

1 or 2 racks of veal, allowing for 2 ribs per person, with the thick skin and most of the fat removed

1kg baby leeks, trimmed and washed

olive oil

1 Throw the shallots, garlic, herbs, butter, and salt and pepper into the bowl of a food processor. Whiz until everything is thoroughly chopped and combined. Remove the blade and mix in the Parmesan and the breadcrumbs. Press the mixture on to the veal racks.

2 Put the baby leeks on a shallow baking tray, drizzle with some olive oil and season with salt and pepper. Place the veal on top of the leeks.

3 Slide the tray on to the third set of runners in the Roasting Oven and cook for 20–30 minutes or until golden and crusty. Serve with the leeks and creamy mashed potatoes.

Conventional Cooking:

Pre-heat the oven to 180°C/350°F/gas 4 and cook for 15–20 minutes, or until cooked to your liking.

wiener schnitzel

serves 4

60g flour

salt and pepper

1 egg, beaten

1 tbsp milk

250g good home-made dried breadcrumbs

4 veal steaks, about 180g each (you can also use pork)

60g beef dripping for frying

1 First, lay out your production line. Put the flour on a flat plate and season it with salt and pepper. Mix the egg and the milk and pour on to another flattish plate. Tip the breadcrumbs on to a third flat plate.

2 Put one steak between two sheets of double thickness cling film and beat it out with a rolling pin or meat mallet until it is about 1cm thick. Repeat for each steak.

3 Place the veal in the seasoned flour and shake off the excess. Next, dip into the egg mix, then finally the breadcrumbs. Pat them in really well.

4 Heat the dripping in a heavy-based frying pan in the bottom of the Roasting Oven, then transfer to the Boiling Plate (moving to the Simmering Plate if it is too fierce), and cook on each side for about 2–3 minutes. They should look golden and crispy.

5 Serve each Weiner schnitzel with a wedge of lemon and boiled potatoes with butter and parsley and a side salad of sweet and sour cabbage (see page 43).

Conventional Cooking:
Cook on the hob.

lamb in a hay box

serves 6–8

**sweet, clean, organic hay –
enough to fill the roasting tin**

1.8–2kg leg of lamb on the bone

**4 garlic cloves, peeled and cut
into slivers**

100g pancetta cubes

6 anchovy fillets, chopped

3 sprigs rosemary

1 tbsp oregano

1 tbsp lemon thyme leaves

olive oil

salt

1 Line the roasting tin with the hay.

2 Make some deep cuts all over the lamb, including the under side, and push the garlic slivers, pancetta cubes, chopped anchovies and herbs into the gashes. Rub the lamb with olive oil and season with salt.

3 Lay the lamb on top of the hay bed, then cover completely with more hay. Cover the tin with a tight fitting lid, or with a triple layer of foil wrapped all around the hay and tin. There must not be any hay exposed or it could catch fire! Put the tin into the Roasting Oven for 1½ hours, then move to the Simmering Oven for another 2–3 hours.

4 Remove the tin from the oven and rest the lamb for 20 minutes, still wrapped in hay. Remove the wrapping and sieve off the pan juices, removing all the excess fat.

5 Serve with the pan juices, fresh spring vegetables and some home-made mint jelly.

Conventional Cooking:
Pre-heat the oven to 180°C/350°F/gas 4 and cook for 2½–3 hours.

Note:
For this recipe it's best to use a really deep roasting tin, preferably with a lid, or cover the tin with foil, as above.

This recipe is something very special and you will have to go to a really good butcher to find the meat. The whole point of this dish is to cook it for the minimum amount of time in order to retain the tenderness and soft texture of the meat. This is the lamb equivalent of veal. If you like your meat well done, don't make this recipe as it will be ruined and you might as well cook an ordinary piece of lamb.

milk-fed lamb with lavender

serves 2–3

4–5 fresh organic hardy lavender leaves, washed

50g unsalted butter, soft

salt

1 leg of milk-fed lamb – it will be pale and tiny, so cook two legs if you want to feed a few more

stock

1 Chop the lavender leaves finely, then mix with the butter and a pinch of salt. Smear the herb butter all over the lamb

2 Put the lamb into a roasting tin and cook in the Roasting Oven for 15 minutes. Move it to the Simmering Oven and cook for another 20 minutes. It will be rare. (The ovens must be up to temperature.)

3 Move the cooked lamb on to a warmed plate and rest. Deglaze the roasting tin with some good stock (not too much) and scrape up all the bits. Serve with the pan juices and some buttered carrots and potatoes.

Conventional Cooking:
Pre-heat the oven to 200°C/400°F/gas 6 and cook the lamb for 15 minutes, then turn the oven down to 160°C/325°F/gas 3, cook for a further 20 minutes and continue as above.

langoustines with garlic and tarragon

serves 4

16 langoustines

100g butter, at room temperature

salt and pepper

1 tbsp chopped fresh tarragon

2 garlic cloves, peeled and crushed

olive oil

1 Put a large shallow baking tray in the Roasting Oven to heat up while you prepare the langoustines.

2 Split the langoustines in half using a sharp knife or scissors.

3 Combine the butter, salt, pepper, tarragon, garlic and a splash of olive oil together in a bowl. Spread on to the langoustine halves.

4 Remove the tray from the oven and place the langoustines on it. Slide back on to the second or third set of runners in the Roasting Oven and cook for 8–10 minutes. You may have to do this in batches. Serve straight away with crusty bread.

Conventional Cooking:
Pre-heat the oven to its hottest temperature and cook as above.

lemon and lime fish cakes

serves 4

500g mashed potatoes (no added butter – see step 1)

500g cod fillet, cut into large chunks

2cm red chilli, deseeded and finely chopped

2cm fresh ginger, grated

1 tbsp fish sauce

1 tbsp chopped fresh coriander

zest of 1 organic lemon

zest and juice of 1 organic lime

1 egg

salt

pepper

sunflower oil, for frying

1 To make mashed potatoes, bring the potatoes up to the boil in a pan of water on the Boiling Plate and boil for 3–4 minutes. Drain off all the water, cover with a tight fitting lid and transfer to the Simmering Oven for 20–30 minutes or until the potatoes are soft. Mash in the usual way.

2 Simply throw all the ingredients except the sunflower oil into a food processor and process until everything is combined but not smooth. Using wet hands, pull off tablespoons of the mix and shape into patties. (At this stage you can chill the fish cakes in the fridge and fry later if you wish. Remove the fish cakes from the fridge at least 20 minutes before cooking.)

3 Heat about 2 tablespoons of oil in a large shallow Bake-O-Glide-lined baking tray on the floor of the Roasting Oven. When it is hot, 'fry' the fish cakes – put the fish cakes on the tray and cook in the Roasting Oven for 15 minutes, then turn over and continue cooking for another 15 minutes or until they are crispy on the outside. Serve on a bed of iceberg lettuce with more wedges of lime and chilli dipping sauce.

Conventional Cooking:
Pre-heat the oven to 220°C/425°F/gas 7 and cook for 30 minutes.

Sorrel flowers from May through to August, but the leaves can be picked as early as February. Its acidic taste makes it a wonderful ingredient in green sauce to accompany meat or fish, made in a similar way to mint sauce. You can also use it in salads and soups and it can be gathered in the wild.

roasted salmon with sorrel and capers

serves 8

60g butter, plus extra for greasing

4–5 sorrel leaves, chopped

salt and pepper

1 organic wild salmon, about 2.5kg, ready to be cooked

FOR THE SAUCE:

3 tbsp natural yoghurt

1 tbsp organic mayonnaise

2 tbsp capers, rinsed

2 sorrel leaves

juice and zest of 1 lime

salt and pepper

1 Mix the butter with about half of the chopped sorrel leaves and season with salt and pepper.

2 Line a large shallow baking tray with enough foil so that the fish can be wrapped up. Grease the foil with some butter. Sprinkle the rest of the chopped sorrel leaves over the foil. Lay the fish on the sorrel leaves and make three slashes on its side. Smear the butter mix into the slashes and into the cavity of the fish. Season with salt and pepper.

3 This step is vital! Measure the girth of the salmon with a tape measure at the widest point to work out the cooking time. Allow 4 minutes cooking for every 2.5cm.

4 Wrap up the fish and cook in the Roasting Oven for the calculated time. The fish is cooked when the skin and dorsal fin pull away easily and the flesh is opaque.

5 While the fish is cooking, put all the sauce ingredients into a food processor and whiz. Check the seasoning and serve with the fish.

Conventional Cooking:
Pre-heat the oven to 180°C/350°F/gas 4 and roast the salmon allowing 5 minutes per 2.5cm.

trout with fennel

serves 4

2–3 good-sized bulbs of fennel, with their tops on

1 organic lemon

175g unsalted butter, at room temperature, plus extra for greasing

salt and pepper

4 trout, gutted and ready for the oven

Pernod

FOR THE SAUCE:

double cream

juice of 1 lemon

25–30g butter or leftover fennel butter from the trout

1 Remove the tops from the fennel and chop finely. Grate the zest of the lemon and put with the fennel tops. Cream the fennel tops and lemon zest with the butter and season with some salt and pepper. Slice the fennel bulbs very thinly.

2 Spread the inside of each trout with some of the fennel butter. (If you have any butter left over, use it to finish the sauce in step 5.) Stuff the trout with half the fennel slices.

3 Line a shallow baking tray with a large piece of foil – enough to be able to cover the top and envelop the fish. Butter the foil, scatter with the rest of the fennel slices and lay the trout on top. Splash over some Pernod, season with salt and pepper and cover with the foil to make a tight parcel.

4 Bake on the third set of runners in the Roasting Oven for 10–15 minutes or until the fish is firm to the touch. Move the fish to a warmed plate, but reserve the juices for the sauce.

5 Pour the juices from the cooked fish into a saucepan and heat up on the Simmering Plate. Add about 4 tablespoons of cream and the juice of a lemon. Heat until simmering, then reduce the sauce for about 1–2 minutes so that it thickens. Whisk in the butter or any leftover fennel butter and season to taste. Serve the trout with the sauce and new potatoes.

Conventional Cooking:
Pre-heat the oven to 180°C/350°F/gas 4 and cook the trout for 10–12 minutes. Finish the sauce on the hob.

little brown trout with hazelnuts

serves 6

3 tbsp flour

salt and pepper

6 fresh trout, gutted and ready for the oven

240ml milk

160g butter

1 tsp grapeseed oil

1 tbsp hazelnut oil

2 tbsp chopped fresh flat leaf parsley

3 tbsp chopped roasted hazelnuts

zest and juice of 1 lemon

1 Season the flour with some salt and pepper and spoon it on to a flat dish. Dip the trout into the milk and then into the flour. Coat well, shaking off the excess flour.

2 Heat 60g of the butter with the grapeseed oil in a large frying pan on the Simmering Plate until frothing. Add as many trout as the pan will take, then transfer the pan to the floor of the Roasting Oven and fry the trout in batches so the pan is not overcrowded for about 3–5 minutes each side (add more butter if necessary) until crispy. Check the fish to make sure the butter does not burn. Set aside on a serving dish and keep warm.

3 Heat the hazelnut oil in a clean pan on the Simmering Plate until hot, add the remaining butter, parsley, hazelnuts, lemon zest, juice, salt and pepper and cook for 1 minute, then pour over the brown trout and serve.

Conventional Cooking:
Use a frying pan on the hob.

fish dusting powder

Take an orange and peel it very thinly, leaving as much white pith behind as possible. Do the same with a lime and a lemon. Put them on to a shallow baking tray lined with Bake-O-Glide and add half a vanilla pod. Dry it out in the Simmering Oven for an hour or so, then move to the protected Simmering Plate lid and leave overnight until really dry. Grind in a coffee grinder and sieve so that it is really fine. Shake it over all sorts of fish before cooking to give it an extra zing!

roasted asparagus with dippy eggs and parmesan

serves 6

3–5 asparagus spears per person, depending on size, woody ends trimmed off

olive oil

salt and pepper

6 organic eggs

100g Parmesan cheese, shaved with a potato peeler

1 Place a rigid grill pan on the floor of the Roasting Oven to heat up. When it is smoking, move it to the Boiling Plate and add the asparagus spears. Drizzle with olive oil and season with salt and pepper. Cook the spears for 2–3 minutes or until they are tender when poked with the point of a knife and are slightly charred with the grill pan marks. Place them on a warmed plate, cover with foil and keep warm.

2 Lift the lid of the Simmering Plate and place a piece of Bake-O-Glide on the hot surface. Lightly grease the Bake-O-Glide with a little olive oil and crack the eggs directly on to the hot surface – you should be able to cook three eggs at a time, or more if they are small. Cook for 1–2 minutes with the lid down.

3 Divide the asparagus between six warm plates and as soon as the first lot of eggs is ready, top each bundle of spears with an egg. Scatter over some Parmesan and drizzle with a little olive oil. The idea is to dip each asparagus spear into the egg yolk.

Conventional Cooking:
Cook the asparagus on the hob. Cook the eggs in a frying pan on the hob.

roasted vegetables in batter

serves 6

3 red onions, peeled and cut in half lengthways, or in quarters if they are large

2 bulbs of fennel, trimmed and cut into wedges

4 baby carrots

8 baby leeks

1 tbsp fresh thyme leaves

salt and pepper

olive oil

FOR THE BATTER:

175g plain flour

3 eggs

175ml milk

110ml water

salt and pepper

½ tbsp fresh thyme leaves

40ml grapeseed oil

1 To make the batter, sift the flour into the eggs and whisk, then slowly add the milk and water, whisking continuously. Season with salt and pepper and add the thyme. Set aside.

2 Put the onions, fennel, carrots, leeks, thyme, salt and pepper into a bowl and pour over about 2 tablespoons of olive oil. Toss the vegetables so they are well coated and tip them into a shallow baking tray.

3 Hang the tray on the second set of runners in the Roasting Oven and roast for about 40–45 minutes until they are charred around the edges and tender. Check them after 25 minutes – if the carrots and fennel are cooked, remove them and set aside until the other vegetables are done. Set aside.

4 When the vegetables are ready, put the grapeseed oil into a small tin and heat it up in the Roasting Oven until it is smoking hot. Move the tin to the Simmering Plate and pour in the batter. Spoon in the roasted vegetables and hang the tin on the third set of runners in the Roasting Oven and cook for about 20–40 minutes, or until the batter has risen and is golden brown. Serve with sour cream with chopped chives stirred into it.

Conventional Cooking:
Pre-heat the oven to 220°C/425°F/gas 7 and cook as above.

Note:
The jury is still out about whether one should or shouldn't let batter stand for a few hours. To get ahead I usually make my batter the day before, but if I'm pushed for time it stands for as long as it take the fat to get up to temperature – the choice is yours.

baked egg with potted shrimps

serves 1

50g potted shrimps
1 tbsp double cream
Tabasco sauce
salt and pepper
fresh tarragon
1 large, firm, slightly under-ripe
beefsteak tomato
1 medium egg

1 Remove the shrimps from the tub and carefully separate the clarified butter from the shrimps. Put the butter into a bowl and melt at the back of the Aga.
2 Put the shrimps into a bowl and separate gently with a fork. Mix in the double cream and season with some Tabasco sauce, salt and pepper and a few chopped fresh tarragon leaves.
3 Cut off the top of the tomato about halfway down from the stem end and carefully scoop out the seeds. Try not to break or split the tomato. Brush the inside of the tomato with the melted butter and season with a little salt and pepper. Spoon the creamy shrimp mix into the tomato, then break the egg on to the mix. Set the tomato on a baking tray.
4 Slide the tray on to the third set of runners in the Roasting Oven and cook for 5–8 minutes or until the egg is cooked. (Make sure the tomato is under-ripe – too ripe and it may split on baking.)
5 Remove from the oven and place the baked tomato on to a dish. Garnish with fresh tarragon leaves and serve with rocket and warm bread.

Conventional Cooking:
Pre-heat the oven to 200°C/400°F/gas 6 and cook as above.

There's nothing better than fresh eggs baked in butter, served with a grating of Parmesan and Melba toast. If making this for a number of people, cook the egg dishes on a shallow baking tray. Pre-heat the tray in the oven before you put the dishes on to it. You will need those flat round white ovenproof porcelain dishes with little bumps on the side for handles.

classic baked eggs

1 tbsp white wine vinegar
3 tbsp grapeseed oil
salt and pepper
chives
unsalted butter
double cream
1 large egg per person
Parmesan cheese

1 To make the dressing, whisk together the vinegar and oil and season with salt and pepper. Snip in some chives.
2 Butter the small dishes. Pour about 1 tablespoon of cream into each, then break the egg on top of the cream. Season with salt and pepper.
3 Bake on the third set of runners in the Roasting Oven for about 3 minutes or until the egg yolk is still soft but the white is cooked. Remove from the oven, shave some Parmesan over the egg and pass round the dressing.

Conventional Cooking:
Pre-heat the oven to 220°C/425°F/gas 7 and cook as above.

baked eggs with potted shrimps

potato gnocchi

serves 4

800g floury potatoes, washed
100g unsalted butter
160g plain flour
1 egg (optional)
salt
40g Parmesan cheese

1 Put the grid shelf on the floor of the Roasting Oven and place the potatoes on it. Bake the potatoes for 40–60 minutes or until they are really soft.
2 Put the butter into a small heatproof bowl and leave it to melt at the back of the Aga.
3 Cut each potato in half and scoop out the flesh, leaving the skin behind (discard or use to make crispy potato skins and eat them with a dip).
4 Put the potato flesh through a potato ricer (I drop mine directly on to a large wooden board) or mash until smooth. Sift over the flour and mix in the egg if using (sometimes I use the whole egg, some times just a whisked egg white), season with some salt and combine it quickly to form a smooth, soft dough.
5 Roll the dough into sausage shapes, about 2cm wide. Cut the 'sausages' into 3cm long pieces. Press a fork into each gnocchi to make little ridges.
6 Bring a large pan of salted water up to a rapid boil on the Boiling Plate, add the gnocchi and cook for 3 minutes or until they rise up to the surface. Remove with a slotted spoon into a warmed dish. Drain off any excess water. Pour over the melted butter, leaving behind any white sediment, and grate over the Parmesan cheese. Gently toss. Check the seasoning and serve.

Conventional Cooking:
Bake the potatoes in an oven pre-heated to 200°C/400°F/gas 6. Cook the gnocchi on the hob.

spring pizza

See page 132 for the basic pizza dough recipe, method and cooking instructions. This is my list of suggested spring toppings, but feel free to invent your own seasonal combination.

baby leeks
fennel
Mozzarella cheese
ramsom leaves, finely chopped
(see page 20)
ricotta cheese
Parmesan cheese

spinach with pine nuts and raisins

serves 6–8

90g raisins

100g pine nuts

90g butter

2kg fresh spinach, washed thoroughly

freshly grated nutmeg

salt and pepper

1 Soak the raisins in boiling water for at least 10 minutes.

2 Lay the pine nuts on a shallow baking tray and toast them in the Roasting Oven for 2–3 minutes, but watch them so they don't burn. Set aside.

3 Place a large, high-sided frying pan on the Simmering Plate and melt the butter. Quickly toss in all the spinach and move it around the pan – it will look as though it won't fit but it will shrink down a lot. You may have to move the pan to the Boiling Plate if you need a bit more heat. If there is a lot of liquid left in the pan, drain most away.

4 When it is cooked, which will only take a few minutes, drain the raisins and toss them in along with the pine nuts and a small grating of nutmeg. Season with salt and pepper and serve.

Conventional Cooking:
Cook on the hob.

Note:
This spinach is great with veal. You can also add the smallest dash of Pernod which takes this dish to a different level, or make it with winter greens, but you may have to chop the leaves up and remove any tough bits.

pickled white cabbage

white cabbage

salt

sugar

white wine or cider vinegar

white pepper

sunflower or grapeseed oil

1 Remove and discard the core of the cabbage. Slice the cabbage leaves very thinly – a food processor is good for this. Set aside.

2 In a small bowl, put in some salt (roughly 1 teaspoon) and almost double the amount of sugar. Pour over about 3 tablespoons vinegar, some white pepper and a dash of oil. Whisk well and taste. This is a very vinegary dressing – it should taste sweet with a hint of sharpness.

3 Put the cabbage into a large bowl and pour over the dressing. The dressing should drown the cabbage so you will have to make up a quantity to suit the amount of cabbage you are using. Cover with cling film and let it all marinate. To serve, you want a small pile on the plate, not a huge portion.

Note:
This recipe is a bit of an assembly job and is done to taste, so precise measurements are not essential. It must be made at least 24 hours ahead of time. Serve this with Weiner schnitzel (see page 28).

Use baby spinach for salads as well as a cooked vegetable. My rule is to never plunge spinach into water, but to melt butter and quickly toss it around the pan. After cooking try and squeeze out as much water as possible.

When I was a child, every Saturday we went to a restaurant called the Burghoff in Chicago and I would always have a salad with their sweet and sour house dressing and delicious creamed spinach – an odd choice for a child. Nick, our waiter, knew our order off by heart as only my mother would change her mind every few weeks. My father always had Weiner schnitzel and a salad with house dressing. There were two breads, rye and pumpernickel, served with everything. I can taste it as I write!

creamed spinach

serves 4

½ onion, peeled and finely chopped

300ml cream

1 bay leaf

salt and pepper

freshly grated nutmeg

knob of butter

500g fresh spinach, washed and stalks removed

50g unsalted butter

25g flour

1 First infuse the onion with the cream. Pour the cream into a saucepan and add the onion, bay leaf, some salt and pepper and a grating of nutmeg. Bring almost to a boil on the Simmering Plate and then set aside.

2 Put a knob of butter into a non-stick frying pan and melt on the Simmering Plate, then toss in the spinach and cook for 3–5 minutes until it has wilted. Remove from the pan and drain in a fine sieve. Squeeze out the excess liquid and chop up the spinach really well.

3 Make the sauce on the Simmering Plate. Remove the bay leaf from the cream. Melt the 50g butter in a saucepan and stir in the flour to make a roux. Cook the flour for a few minutes, then add the warm cream little by little, stirring all the time so the sauce is smooth and silky (although it still has the onion in it).

4 When all the cream has been added and the sauce is ready, simmer gently for a few more minutes. Stir in the chopped spinach and continue to cook for 1 minute. Taste for seasoning, give it a quick grind of nutmeg and serve.

Conventional Cooking:
Cook on the hob.

Purple sprouting broccoli is not so fashionable as it once was, but I like it more than bog-standard broccoli and we grow it in our garden. It is great for stir-frying.

purple sprouting broccoli with potted shrimps

purple sprouting broccoli
potted shrimps

1 Bring a pan of water up to the boil on the Boiling Plate. Drop in the purple sprouting broccoli and cook for a few minutes. I like it still with a bit of bite. Drain and put into a dish.

2 Take the potted shrimps and break them up with a fork. Toss in with the broccoli and fold everything together so all the butter from the shrimps melts. Serve straight away.

Conventional Cooking:
Cook on the hob.

Note:
During my workshops there is always lots of chatter and recipe swapping, and this was one passed on to me by a lady from Yorkshire. This is not really a recipe as such – more a 'how to' as you can adjust the quantities to suit.

roasted cauliflower with pancetta and taleggio

serves 4

100g pancetta slices
1 cauliflower head, divided into florets
olive oil
pepper
50g Taleggio cheese, sliced

1 Fry the pancetta slices in a small roasting tin on the floor of the Roasting Oven or on the Simmering Plate until crispy. Remove from the tin and set aside. Remove all but ½ tablespoon of the fat.

2 Put the cauliflower florets into a bowl and toss them in 1 tablespoon olive oil. Season with some pepper.

3 Tip the cauliflower into the roasting tin and cook on the third set of runners in the Roasting Oven for 12–15 minutes or until soft but slightly charred. Remove from the oven and scatter over the slices of cheese. Return to the oven for a few minutes until the cheese starts to melt. Crumble over the pancetta and serve.

Conventional Cooking:
Fry the pancetta on the hob. Pre-heat the oven to 200°C/400°F/gas 6 and bake as above.

Spring carrots are sweet and fresh tasting and are delicious raw with a dip. They should never be peeled, only washed or brushed of their soil. I have to say organic carrots are wonderful – when I visited an organic farm this year, we ate them straight out of the ground and they were superb. Look for bright green tops when you are buying them, I like to leave a bit of the green top showing and I also only cook them briefly as I prefer my vegetables on the raw side.

baby carrots glazed with balsamic butter

serves 4

40g unsalted butter, at room temperature
2 tbsp aged balsamic vinegar
salt
2 leaves wild garlic, chopped
pinch of sugar
750g baby spring carrots, with a little bit of green top on

1 Beat the butter, balsamic vinegar, salt, wild garlic leaves and sugar together until combined. Set aside.
2 Put the baby carrots into a saucepan of water and bring to the boil on the Boiling Plate. Cook for 2–3 minutes. Drain off all the water and add the balsamic butter. Put a lid on and transfer to the Simmering Oven for 10–15 minutes. Serve.

Conventional Cooking:
Take a disc of waxed paper and cut it to fit the circumference of your saucepan. Cut a small hole in the centre. Put the carrots into the saucepan and add about 3cm of water and the butter glaze mix. Push the paper down on to the carrots, bring to a rapid simmer over a medium heat and cook for 6–8 minutes.

I was taught to make crème brûlée on the hob, not in a bain-marie. If you have success making it another way, then my advice is to carry on – I just try to avoid boiling water coming out of ovens in trays – too dangerous for me! I also must stress that, try as you might, you will not brûlée the top with an Aga. The blow-torch is the Aga owner's friend and I use mine for browning whenever I think something needs a little extra colour.

crème brûlée

serves 6–8, depending on the size of your ramekins

600ml double cream – the very best you can find

1 vanilla pod, or 1 tsp vanilla extract

1 tbsp golden caster sugar (you could add another ½ tbsp sugar if you wish, but I prefer less because of the burnt sugar on top)

9 large organic egg yolks

4 tbsp Demerara sugar

bottle of water with a fine mist or spray attachment

1 Place the ramekins in the freezer.

2 Make the custard. Put the cream into a non-stick saucepan. Split the vanilla pod with a sharp knife and scrape out the seeds and add the bean and all the seeds to the cream, or add the vanilla extract. Bring the cream up to a simmer on the Simmering Plate. Do not let it boil.

3 Whisk the caster sugar and egg yolks together in a large bowl until they are thick.

4 Pour the cream on to the egg mixture little by little, whisking all the time. Clean the saucepan and dry.

5 When all the cream is stirred into the egg mix, pour it through a sieve back into the clean non-stick pan. Return the pan to the Simmering Plate and stir until thick, about 8–10 minutes. Do not boil. Pour into the ice-cold ramekins and leave to set in the fridge overnight.

6 When you are ready to brûlée them, spread the Demerara sugar in an even layer over each ramekin. Spray the surface of the sugar with a little water, then using a blow torch, blast away. Ideally you should give them another 20–30 minutes in the fridge before serving.

Conventional Cooking
Make on the hob over a low heat.

milk and honey jelly

serves 6

grapeseed oil

580ml gold top Jersey milk

85ml double cream – the best
you can buy but not too thick

160ml honey – one with a floral
base note

2 vanilla pods, split

4 leaves gelatine

1 You will need either individual ramekins or a 20.5cm jelly mould. Lightly grease the ramekins or bowl with tasteless oil, such as grapeseed.

2 Put about 4 tablespoons of the milk into a flattish bowl and soak the gelatine leaves in it so that they become very soft.

3 Put the rest of the milk, cream, honey and split vanilla pods into a saucepan and gently heat on the Simmering Plate so they just reach a gentle simmer.

4 Remove from the heat and stir in the soaking gelatine and any of the remaining soaking milk. Strain the mix through a sieve into the jelly mould. Cover with cling film and refrigerate overnight.

5 To serve, dip the base of the mould in hot water and gently squeeze the mould if it is plastic or coax it out with a gentle push of clean fingers. Invert a plate over the top of the mould and shake to release the jelly. Serve with fresh fruit.

Conventional Cooking:
Cook on the hob.

panna cotta

serves 6

1.2 litres double cream
2 vanilla pods, split
**thinly pared rind of 2 organic
lemons (optional)**
3 gelatine leaves
150ml milk
100g icing sugar

1 Pour 900ml of the cream into a pan and add the vanilla and lemon rind. Bring to the boil on the Boiling Plate, then move to the Simmering Plate and simmer until it is reduced to one third. Remove the lemon rind and set aside. Squeeze the vanilla seeds out and remove the pod.

2 Soak the gelatine leaves in the milk until soft. Remove the gelatine and set aside. Heat the milk in a saucepan on the Boiling Plate until boiling, then remove from the heat, add the gelatine back in and stir until it has dissolved. (This recipe produces a soft set, so don't worry if it spreads a little when turned out. If you want it to stand upright, use an extra gelatine leaf.)

3 Pour the hot milk into the hot cream, stir and sieve into a bowl. Leave to cool completely.

4 Whip the remaining cream with the icing sugar and fold it into the cooled cream/milk mix. Divide the reserved lemon rind between six small bowls and pour in the panna cotta. Cover and allow to set in the fridge. Turn out on to plates and serve with baked rhubarb (see below).

Conventional Cooking:
Cook on the hob.

Rhubarb is technically a vegetable, but most of us see it as a fruit. It is related to sorrel so has a slight acidic taste which balances out when combined with sugar.

baked rhubarb

serves 6

1.4kg rhubarb
150g golden caster sugar
3cm ginger root, finely grated

1 Cut the rhubarb into chunks and put into an ovenproof gratin dish. Sprinkle over the sugar and grated ginger.

2 Bake in the Simmering Oven for 40–60 minutes or until soft. You can speed things up by baking it in the Roasting Oven for 10 minutes, then moving it to the Simmering Oven. For 4-oven Aga owners, bake in the Baking Oven for 30–40 minutes. Allow to cool, then serve.

Conventional Cooking:
Pre-heat the oven to 160°C/325°F/gas 3 and bake for 30 minutes.

Note:
For rhubarb and ginger fool, whiz cold baked rhubarb in a food processor to a purée. Fold in 400ml whipped double cream (or thick natural yoghurt for a zingier taste), add chopped crystallised ginger pieces, stir and chill.

panna cotta with baked rhubarb

baked ricotta cheesecake

serves 6–8

grapeseed oil
100g golden caster sugar
200g lemon curd
1kg ricotta cheese
1 tsp vanilla extract
4 eggs, beaten
32g plain flour, sifted
zest of 2 organic lemons
50ml Limoncello, or lemon juice if you can't find it
icing sugar, for dusting

1 Lightly grease an 18cm springform tin with grapeseed oil.

2 Put the sugar and lemon curd into a food processor and process until smooth. Add all the rest of the ingredients, apart from the icing sugar, and process until well combined and smooth.

3 Pour into the prepared tin and bake in the Roasting Oven on the Cold Plain Shelf for about 15 minutes, then transfer the tin and the shelf to the Simmering Oven for about 1 hour. It should still have a wobbly centre when you take it out. Keep an eye on it as you do not want to end up with a firm set coming out of the oven. Remove it from the oven and leave to cool.

4 Remove from the tin and dust with icing sugar. Serve with fresh fruit.

Conventional Cooking:
Pre-heat the oven to 160°C/325°F/gas 3 and cook as above.

fairy cakes

makes 6

100g unsalted butter, at room temperature
100g self-raising flour
100g golden caster sugar
1 tsp baking powder
2 eggs

FOR THE ICING:
225g icing sugar
2–4 tbsp water or milk
1 packet of dolly mixture sweets

1 Line a shallow muffin tin with paper cases.

2 Beat all the cake ingredients together in an electric mixer. Spoon the mix into the paper cases so they are half full.

3 Place the muffin tin inside a roasting tin and slide the tin onto the third or fourth set of runners in the Roasting Oven and bake for 15–20 minutes or until the cakes have risen and are golden on top. Remove from the tin and cool on a wire rack.

4 To make the icing, mix the icing sugar and liquid and beat until smooth. Spoon onto the cakes and top with the sweets.

Conventional Cooking:
Pre-heat the oven to 200°C/400°F/gas 6 and bake the cakes directly in the muffin tin (don't put them into another tin).

Note:
To make chocolate fairy cakes, instead of 100g flour, use 75g self-raising flour and 25g cocoa powder.

summer

what's in season?

June

Fruit
Apricots
  (mid-summer to
  early autumn)
Cherries
Currants
  (red/white/black)
Figs
Gooseberries
Pears
Raspberries
Strawberries

Vegetables
Asparagus
Beetroot
Broad beans
Carrots
Cucumbers
Early Jersey
  potatoes
Florence fennel
Globe artichokes
Lettuce
Peas
Radishes
Rhubarb
Spinach
Tomatoes
Watercress

Herbs
Basil
Chives
Elderflowers
Horseradish
Sorrel

Fish and seafood
Cod
Crab

Lemon sole
Lobster
Mackerel
Scallops
Sea bass
Spider crab
Tuna
Wild brown trout
Wild salmon

Meat
Lamb

Dairy
Cheese
  (Coulommiers,
  Feta, Gorgonzola,
  Mozzarella, Ricotta,
  Waterloo)

July

Fruit
Apples
Apricots
Blueberries
Cherries
Currants
  (red/white/black)
Figs
Gooseberries
Loganberries
Mulberries
Pears
Plums
Raspberries
Rhubarb
Strawberries
Wild strawberries

Vegetables
Aubergines
Beetroot
Broccoli
Broad beans
Calabrese
Carrots
Chanterelles
Courgettes
Florence fennel
French beans
Garlic (fresh)
Globe artichokes
Lettuce
New potatoes
Onions (fresh)
Peas
Radish
Runner beans
Samphire
Summer truffles
Tomatoes
Watercress
Wild fennel

Herbs
Elderflowers
Horseradish
Rocket
Sorrel

Fish and seafood
Crab
Crayfish
Lobster
Scallops
Sea bass
Sea trout

Meat
Rabbit
Wood pigeon

Dairy
Cheese
  (Coulommiers,
  Feta, Gorgonzola,
  Mozzarella, Ricotta,
  Waterloo)

August

Fruit
Apples
Apricots
Bilberries
Blackberries
Blueberries
Cherries
Figs
Greengages
Loganberries
Melons
Mulberries
Nectarines
Peaches
Pears
Raspberries (summer
  crop coming to an
  end, autumn crop
  starting)
Wild strawberries

Vegetables
Aubergines
Beans (coming to
  an end)
Calabrese
Carrots
Ceps
Chanterelles
Chard
Chillies
Courgettes

Cucumbers
Field mushrooms
Garlic
Globe artichokes
Lettuce
Marrows
Onions
Oyster mushrooms
Peppers
Potatoes (new main
  crop)
Puffballs
Radishes
Rocket
Sorrel
Spinach
Summer truffles
Sweetcorn
Tomatoes
Watercress

Herbs
You name it – it's
  available

Nuts
Hazelnuts

Meat
Grouse
Snipe

Fish and seafood
Crab
Lobster
Mackerel
Scallops
Sea bass
Squid

summer recipes

Soups and Starters
Chilled Broad Bean and Mint Soup
Ribollita
Corn-off-the-Cob
Grilled Aubergine Pâté
Courgette Fritters
Smoked Salmon and Potato Blinis

Main Courses/Meat
Roast Grouse with Quince Cheese
Amy's Summer Chicken
Summer Roasted Chicken with Bread
   Salad
Chicken with Fresh Summer Peas
Lemon and Rosemary Chicken
Leg of Lamb with Lemon and Rosemary
Minted Bread Sauce
Butterflied Lamb with Baby Fennel

Main Courses/Fish
Sea Bass Baked in Foil
Crab Tart
Pan-fried Scallops with Chilli and Lemon
   on Spaghetti
Isle of Wight Kitchen Clam Bake
Lobster Rolls

Main Courses/Vegetarian
Baked Corn-on-the-Cob with Roasted
   Garlic Butter
Summer Pizza
Lemon Risotto
Broad Beans with Pasta and Ricotta

Accompaniments
Roasted Shallots
Balsamic Roasted Beetroot
Peas with Lettuce and Prosciutto
Hot Potato Salad
Sautéed Courgettes with Basil and Mint
Summer Fennel Slaw

Desserts and Baking
Cream Cheese Lemon Roulade
Seasonal Crumble Tart
Summer Tarts
Cherry Gratin
Summer Victoria Sponge
Blueberry and Peach Cake
Focaccia al Formaggio
Cherry Focaccia Bread

Preserves and Drinks
Basic Chutney
Tomato and Chilli Chutney
Bread and Butter Pickles
Red Onion Confit
Mint Sauce
Deluxe Mint Sauce
Tomato Ketchup
Sicilian Lemon Relish
Fruits Steeped in Liqueurs
Lemon Verbena Tisane
Green Apple Tea
Vin d'Orange
Elderflower Cordial
Lemon Verbena Cordial
Rose Petal Confiture

chilled broad bean and mint soup

serves 4

1.5kg broad beans, plus a handful for garnish

1 litre good quality stock

1 garlic clove, peeled

salt and pepper

2 tbsp finely chopped mint

1 tbsp torn basil

2 tbsp crème fraîche

50 g Parmesan cheese

olive oil, for serving

1 Have a bowl of iced water ready for blanching. Shell the beans from the tough pod. Bring a pan of water up to the boil on the Boiling Plate and cook the beans in salted boiling water for 2–3 minutes or until they start to wrinkle and they still have a bit of bite to them. Remove the beans with a slotted spoon and plunge them into the iced water immediately. Drain from the iced water, carefully peel off the membrane and put the bright green beans into a bowl. This can be done in advance.

2 Put the stock and garlic into a saucepan, season well with salt and pepper and bring it up to a simmer on the Simmering Plate. Gently simmer for about 2 minutes.

3 Add the prepared broad beans, then take off the heat and add the herbs and crème fraîche, then liquidise using a blender or food processor. Leave to chill in the fridge.

4 Check the seasoning and serve with a few of the reserved beans, a shaving of the Parmesan, a drizzle of olive oil and crusty bread.

Conventional Cooking:
Cook on the hob.

Note:
When you are serving something chilled, you must season it well with salt as the taste will dull in the chilling process.

Borlotti beans really are well worth growing if you have the space in your garden. Apart from their delicious taste, they look great too. Never cook any beans in salted water as it toughens their skins.

ribollita

serves 8–10

1.5kg fresh borlotti beans

6 garlic cloves, peeled

1.5kg fresh tomatoes, skinned and chopped (leave one tomato whole, for step 1)

handful of flat leaf parsley

500g spinach

500g summer chard

olive oil

3 stalks celery, finely chopped

2 onions, peeled and finely chopped

1 large handful of basil

2 tbsp fresh oregano leaves

salt and pepper

1 large loaf sourdough bread

180g Parmesan cheese, grated

1 Remove the borlotti beans from their pods, discarding any brown beans. Put them in a saucepan and cover with cold water. Add three garlic cloves, one whole tomato, half the flat leaf parsley and all the parsley stalks. Bring up to the boil on the Boiling Plate for 5 minutes. Cover the saucepan with a lid and transfer to the Simmering Oven for 45 minutes or until the beans are soft. Drain and set aside. Also set one of these cooked garlic cloves aside for use in step 5.

2 Bring a pan of water up to the boil on the Boiling Plate and blanch the spinach for 1 minute, drain and chop. Do the same to the chard.

3 Put a large deep casserole on the Simmering Plate and heat up some olive oil. Soften the celery and onion, then add the remaining garlic and crush when soft. Add the chopped tomatoes and about four spoonfuls of beans and crush them with a potato masher. Add the rest of the beans and the remaining herbs. Season with salt and pepper. Add enough water to just cover the vegetables plus 500ml more, and bring up to the boil on the Boiling Plate. Take off the heat.

4 Slice the loaf of bread. Layer half the bread and the soup into a large ovenproof dish or bowl, starting and ending with the bread so that it forms the top layer. Cover with foil or a lid and cook in the Roasting Oven for about 1 hour.

5 Meanwhile, rub the remaining bread slices with the reserved garlic clove.

6 Remove the soup from the oven 20 minutes before you want to serve it. Top with the rest of the bread and sprinkle over the Parmesan cheese. Return to the oven uncovered until the bread is crispy and the cheese melting. Serve in bowls.

Conventional Cooking:
Prepare the soup on the hob. Pre-heat the oven to 200°C/400°F/gas 6 and cook as above.

corn-off-the-cob

serves 6

6 ears of fresh corn

25g butter

1 tbsp light olive oil

1 onion, peeled and finely chopped

1 level tbsp plain flour

240ml chicken stock

240ml crème fraîche

40g freshly grated Parmesan cheese, plus more to serve

salt and pepper

2 tbsp chopped fresh flat leaf parsley

1 tbsp chopped chives

wild rocket

1 Remove the kernels from the corncobs into a bowl (scraping all of the milky pulp into the bowl as well).

2 Heat the butter and oil in a large pan on the Simmering Plate. When melted, add the onion, then move the pan to the floor of the Roasting Oven until the onions are soft but not coloured.

3 Place the pan back on the Simmering Plate and add the kernels and flour. Stir to coat evenly. Pour in the chicken stock and bring to the boil stirring all the time. Boil until the liquid is reduced by half, then add the crème fraîche and cook for another 3–4 minutes, until creamy.

4 Take the pan off the heat, stir in the Parmesan, season with salt and pepper and add the herbs. Spoon on to warmed plates. Sprinkle over some more Parmesan and a little wild rocket.

Conventional Cooking:
Cook on the hob.

grilled aubergine pâté

serves 6–8

3 medium sized aubergines

1 organic lemon

salt and pepper

ground cumin – just enough to cover the tip of a knife

sunflower oil

1 Place the aubergines on a grill rack that will fit into one of your roasting tins. Roast them in the Roasting Oven for 15–20 minutes or until the skin is blistered and black.

2 Remove them from the tin and place them into a plastic bag. Seal the bag and leave for 20 minutes or so. You want the aubergines to sweat. Put on some rubber gloves, undo the plastic bag and peel off the skin and discard.

3 Put the aubergine flesh into a nylon sieve and push out as much liquid as possible. Put the drained flesh into a food processor and add the zest of the lemon and a little squeeze of juice. Add the spice and salt and pepper and blitz away. Gradually add 3–4 tablespoons of the sunflower oil until the pâté is smooth.

4 Check the seasoning and pour the pâté into a dish. Cover with cling film and chill. Serve with toasted pitta bread, lemon wedges and chopped flat leaf parsley sprinkled over the top.

Conventional Cooking:
Pre-heat the oven to 200°C/400°F/gas 6 and bake the aubergine as above.

courgette fritters

makes about 20 small fritters

8–10 small courgettes
1 large carrot, peeled
1 medium sweet onion, peeled
1 very waxy potato, peeled
1 large red pepper, deseeded
1 garlic clove, peeled
1 tsp baking powder
5 tbsp plain flour
1 large organic egg
salt and pepper
sunflower oil

1 Grate the courgettes, carrot, onion, potato, red pepper and garlic into a bowl. Squeeze out any excess water with your hands. Return the grated veg to a large bowl and add the baking powder, flour, egg and salt and pepper. Mix well.

2 Place a round piece of Bake-O-Glide on the Simmering Plate and brush with sunflower oil. Drop spoonfuls of the mix on to the Simmering Plate and cook until the fritter edges are crispy – about 2–3 minutes each side. You will have to do this in batches.

3 Drain on kitchen paper and serve hot with blueberry conserve and sour cream, or with apple sauce and crème fraîche.

Conventional Cooking:
Cook in a frying pan over a medium heat on the hob.

Note:
My family makes these all the time and they are soooo good! You can adjust the quantities of vegetables to suit what is available.

smoked salmon and potato blinis

makes 10–14 pancakes, depending on size

FOR THE BLINIS:
100g cold smooth mashed potatoes (no milk or butter added)
1 egg, separated
1 tbsp double cream
1 rounded tbsp self-raising flour
salt and white pepper
sunflower oil

FOR THE TOPPING:
4 tbsp sour cream
1 tbsp chopped chives
75g smoked salmon, cut into strips or chopped
juice of 1 lemon
ground black pepper

1 In a large bowl mix the potato, egg yolk, cream, flour, salt and pepper together. Whisk the egg white in a separate bowl until stiff, then gently fold into the potato mix.

2 Open the lid of the Simmering Plate and place a round piece of Bake-O-Glide on it. Lightly grease with a piece of kitchen paper dipped in some sunflower oil. Wipe it across the Bake-O-Glide and drop spoonfuls of the pancake mix on to the Bake-O-Glide. Cook for 1 minute on each side and remove to a warmed plate.

3 Top each blini with some sour cream mixed with chives, smoked salmon strips, a squeeze of lemon juice and some ground black pepper.

Conventional Cooking:
Make the blinis in a frying pan on the hob.

Note:
A home economist on a TV show I was working on gave me this recipe. The blinis are wonderfully light and good with most things. You can make them two weeks in advance, freeze and then re-heat in the Roasting Oven for 2–3 minutes. For really smooth mashed potatoes, use a potato ricer.

Grouse is eagerly awaited as the first shots of the year hit high on the glorious 12th August. The fashion to hang game until its neck fell off is long gone except in only the most ancient of houses which is a good thing! I like grouse served with quince cheese.

roast grouse with quince cheese

serves 2

1 red onion, peeled and thickly sliced

60g quince cheese (see page 149)

2 grouse, oven ready

30g butter, softened

salt and pepper

2 bay leaves

splash of Marsala wine

150ml good chicken stock

1 Lay the onion slices on the bottom of a roasting tin. Put half the quince cheese into each grouse cavity and season with salt and pepper. Smear the butter over each bird and season with salt and pepper. Lay the grouse over the onions and tuck in the bay leaves.

2 Roast on the third set of runners in the Roasting Oven for 15–20 minutes or until cooked to your liking (some people like their grouse very rare, but not me – I prefer it when the juices run clear when the thigh is poked with a skewer).

3 Remove the birds from the oven. Lift out each bird and carefully tip them so that any quince cheese left in the cavity goes into the pan juices. Move them to a warmed plate, cover with foil and rest while you make the gravy.

4 Skim off excess fat from the tin. Remove the bay leaves. Deglaze the tin with the Marsala, add the stock and bring it all to the boil on the Boiling Plate, then let it simmer for 2–3 minutes. Pour the gravy into a warmed jug. Serve each grouse with a few small roast potatoes and follow with a salad.

Conventional Cooking:
Pre-heat the oven to 220°C/425°F/gas 7 and cook as above. Make the gravy on the hob.

amy's summer chicken

serves 8

1 litre chicken stock and white wine (the ratio of stock to wine is your choice)

8 large chicken breasts

250g cubed pancetta, cooked

500ml crème fraîche

500ml mayonnaise

1 small head celery, thinly sliced

1 handful of basil leaves, torn

200g Parmesan cheese, grated

juice of half a lemon

1 large packet organic vegetable crisps

1 Bring the stock and wine up to the boil in a large pan on the Boiling Plate, place the chicken in the pan, bring back to the boil, then place in the Simmering Oven for 1 hour, or until cooked through. When cooked, take out of the stock and leave to cool. (This can be done the day before, and the stock will now be perfect for making a soup.)

2 Cook the pancetta in a frying pan on the floor of the Simmering Oven.

3 Cut the cooled chicken into chunks.

4 Mix the crème fraîche, mayonnaise, celery, basil, pancetta and half of the cheese in a bowl. Stir in the chicken and lemon juice, season with salt and pepper and spoon into an ovenproof dish. (I put the dish on to a baking tray to avoid spillages!) Crush the vegetable crisps and sprinkle over the chicken, then add the remaining cheese.

5 Bake in the Roasting Oven for 25 minutes or until brown and crispy. Delicious served hot or cold.

Conventional Cooking:

Bring the stock and wine to the boil on the hob, add the chicken, bring back to the boil, then simmer on the hob for 30–40 minutes or until cooked through. Cook the pancetta on the hob. Pre-heat the oven to 180°C/350°F/gas 4 and bake for 30 minutes until browned and hot all the way through.

Note:

This recipe is adapted from one kindly given to me by the St John Ambulance committee for a summer function.

summer roasted chicken with bread salad

serves 6

FOR THE CHICKEN:

2 onions, peeled

4–6 fresh tender sprigs of rosemary, or other herb such as oregano, thyme or sage

1–1.75kg organic free-range chicken, trimmed (ask your butcher to prepare it)

4–5 garlic cloves in their papery cases

sea salt

FOR THE BREAD SALAD:

250g stale ciabatta bread or other rustic bread (the bread should be about 2 days old)

6 tbsp mild olive oil, plus extra for brushing the bread

1 tbsp sultanas

red wine vinegar

2 tbsp toasted pine nuts

2 tbsp white balsamic vinegar

salt and pepper

1 bag of organic rocket

1 head of Cos lettuce, washed and prepared

1 Cut the onions into quarters. Place the rosemary and onions on the bottom of a roasting tin and put the chicken on top of them, breast side up. Scatter round the garlic cloves. Rub the salt over the chicken, then cook in the Roasting Oven for 20 minutes.

2 Remove from the oven and turn the chicken breast side down for another 20 minutes, then flip the chicken over again to crisp up the breast for a further 10–15 minutes or until the leg juices run clear when pierced with a skewer and the skin is very crispy. When the chicken is cooked, let it rest for 10–15 minutes.

3 While the chicken is cooking, make the bread salad. Trim the bread of the crusts and cut into largish chunks. Brush the bread all over with olive oil. Put the bread on a baking tray and into the Roasting Oven and bake for approximately 10 minutes, turning over halfway through so all the pieces are crisp and golden. Some will be cooked more than others. When the bread is ready, tear into uneven pieces.

4 Put the sultanas into a bowl and cover with boiling water and a dash of red wine vinegar. Set aside.

5 To make the dressing, whisk the white balsamic vinegar and olive oil together and season with salt and pepper. Place the bread in a large bowl and dress it with 3 tablespoons of the dressing. Taste and adjust seasoning. Reserve the remaining dressing.

6 Remove the onions and garlic cloves from the roasting tin and set aside. Drain the fat from the roasting tin and reserve the juices in a bowl. Deglaze the pan with a little hot water and add to the juices.

7 Squeeze the garlic cloves out of the paper case and add them and the onions to the bread. Toss in the pine nuts, sultanas, Cos and rocket and then arrange on a large platter. Cut the chicken into pieces and arrange on top of the bread salad. Pour over some of the reserved pan juices. Serve the remaining pan juices and dressing on the side.

Conventional Cooking:

For the chicken, pre-heat the oven to 220°C/425°F/gas 7 and cook as above. Bake the bread at 200°C/400°F/gas 6 as above.

chicken with fresh summer peas

serves 4

olive oil

2 small chickens, jointed into 8 pieces

80g butter

600g fresh shelled peas (you will need to buy at least 1.5kg in the pod)

2 little gem lettuces, cut into 4 long pieces

1 bunch baby spring onions, trimmed and split in half

1 bunch chopped fresh mint, plus extra to serve

1 tbsp golden caster sugar

salt and pepper

100ml home-made chicken stock

1 Heat up some olive oil in a frying pan on the floor of the Roasting Oven and brown the chicken pieces (you will need to do this in batches). I like to do this in the Roasting Oven, but you can also use either the Simmering or Boiling Plates.

2 Melt half of the butter in a large casserole. Put the browned chicken on the bottom of the casserole, then add the peas, lettuce, spring onions, chopped mint, sugar, salt and pepper, then top up with the stock.

3 Bring the casserole up to a boil on the Boiling Plate, then cover and transfer to the Roasting Oven for 35–40 minutes or until the chicken is cooked. Serve with the casserole juices, some more freshly chopped mint and new potatoes.

Conventional Cooking:
Brown the chicken pieces on the hob, then transfer to an oven pre-heated to 180°C/350°F/gas 4 for 40–45 minutes.

lemon and rosemary chicken

serves 6

2 large chickens, jointed into 6 pieces

olive oil

3 stalks of rosemary with the leaves removed and chopped

zest and juice of 2 organic lemons

10 shallots, cut in half – only remove the outer paper if muddy

1 head of garlic, cloves divided but not peeled

250ml sweet white wine

salt and pepper

1 tbsp crème fraîche

1 Put the chicken pieces into a bowl and drizzle about 3–4 tablespoons of olive oil over them. Add the rosemary, lemon zest, shallots, garlic and wine. Season with salt and pepper and rub the mix into the chicken.

2 Tip the contents of the bowl into a large roasting tin. Roast the chickens on the third set of runners in the Roasting Oven for 40–45 minutes or until golden and the shallots are slightly caramelised.

3 Remove the chicken pieces and shallots to a warmed serving platter. Put the garlic cloves into a warm bowl. Set aside and keep warm.

4 Place the tin on the Simmering Plate and pour in the lemon juice, scraping up all the browned bits on the bottom of the tin. Squeeze in a couple of garlic cloves – the pulp inside the papery case will just ooze out. Let the juices thicken for 3–4 minutes, then stir in the crème fraîche, check the seasoning and pour over the chicken. Serve the chicken with the remaining garlic cloves.

Conventional Cooking:
Pre-heat the oven to 220°C/425°F/gas 7 and cook as above. Cook the sauce on the hob.

leg of lamb with lemon and rosemary

serves 6

2.5kg leg of lamb

1 tbsp chopped fresh rosemary, plus 6 whole sprigs

juice and zest of 1 large, juicy lemon

1 head of garlic, unpeeled and cut in half horizontally

salt and pepper

250ml good quality olive oil

2 red onions, peeled and cut in half

1 Put the lamb into a deep bowl or a large resealable plastic bag, then simply add the rosemary, lemon juice and zest, garlic, salt and pepper, and olive oil (be generous with the oil – if you need more to coat the lamb well, then go ahead). Massage the marinade into the lamb really well, using your hands, then cover the bowl or seal the bag and refrigerate for up to 24 hours.

2 Remove the lamb from the fridge at least 30 minutes before cooking. Place the onion halves cut side down in the roasting tin, then rest the lamb on them and pour over the juices from the marinade.

3 Cook the lamb for 40 minutes in the Roasting Oven, then transfer to the Simmering Oven for 2–3 hours or until the meat is done to your liking.

4 When it is ready, remove the leg of lamb from the oven, put the meat on a warm plate and leave to rest for 15 minutes. Remove the onion from the tin and reserve for the bread sauce (see below). Remove the excess fat from the pan juices, then bubble up the pan juices on the Simmering Plate. Scrape up any caramelised bits from the bottom and pour into a warm jug.

Conventional Cooking:

Pre-heat the oven to its hottest setting and roast the lamb, as above, for 25 minutes. Turn the oven down to 150°C/300°F/gas 2 and continue to cook for 1½ hours or until the lamb is done to your liking. Continue as above.

Note:

This is a classic summer dish. Be sure the lamb is of the highest quality and allow enough time for it to marinate. The lamb should be crusty on the outside and tender and juicy on the inside. Serve with the pan juices, minted bread sauce and some broad beans.

minted bread sauce

stale bread

chopped fresh mint

½ tbsp red wine vinegar

½ tsp Dijon mustard

salt and pepper

red onion from the roasted lamb (above), chopped into pieces

about 50ml olive oil

1 tbsp water

1 Remove the crusts from the bread. Tear the bread into small chunks.

2 Put all the ingredients into a bowl and combine thoroughly. Add enough olive oil to just slacken the sauce. I also like to pour in some of the pan juices from the lamb. Taste and adjust the seasoning to your liking.

Note:

Adjust the quantities to suit your taste, using a ratio of three parts mint to one part bread.

butterflied lamb with baby fennel

serves 6

2.5kg leg of lamb, butterflied (this means bone removed – ask your butcher to do this for you)

5–6 baby fennel bulbs, trimmed of any yucky leaves

1 tbsp oregano leaves

1 tbsp basil leaves

juice and zest of 1 large juicy lemon

salt and pepper

1 head of garlic, unpeeled and cut in half horizontally

2 red onions, peeled and cut in half

250ml good-quality olive oil

1 Put the lamb and fennel bulbs in a deep bowl or a large, resealable plastic bag. Add the herbs, lemon juice and zest, salt, pepper, garlic, onions, fennel and olive oil (be generous with the olive oil – if you need more to really coat the leg of lamb, then go ahead)

2 Massage the marinade into the lamb with your hands really well, then cover the bowl or seal the bag and refrigerate for up to 24 hours. Remove from the fridge at least 30 minutes before cooking.

3 Transfer the red onions and fennel bulbs from the marinade bowl or bag to a small roasting tin. Place on the second set of runners in the Roasting Oven and roast for 20–30 minutes or until they are cooked and a little charred around the edges. Remove from the tin and cool.

4 Put some olive oil into the large cast-iron griddle pan and heat on the floor of the Roasting Oven until it is smoking hot. Bring the pan to the Boiling Plate, place the lamb on it and seal the meat on all sides. Pour over the marinade. Put the grid shelf on the floor of the Roasting Oven, place the griddle pan on top and cook the lamb for 30 minutes or until the meat is done to your liking.

5 When it is ready, transfer the lamb to a warm plate, cover tightly with cling film and leave to rest for 15 minutes. Remove excess fat from the pan juices, then bubble up the pan juices on the Simmering Plate, scrape up any caramelised bits from the bottom and pour into a warm jug.

6 Slice the lamb and serve with the cooled roasted fennel and red onions, the pan juices, and some broad beans and crusty bread.

Conventional Cooking:
Pre-heat the oven to its highest setting and cook the lamb for 20 minutes. Turn down the heat to 170°C/340°F/gas 3½ and roast for another 1½ hours or until the meat is done to your liking.

Note:
The lamb should be crusty on the outside but tender and juicy on the inside. It can be served warm or cool and is perfect for picnics. Remember to start this recipe in advance to allow time for marinating.

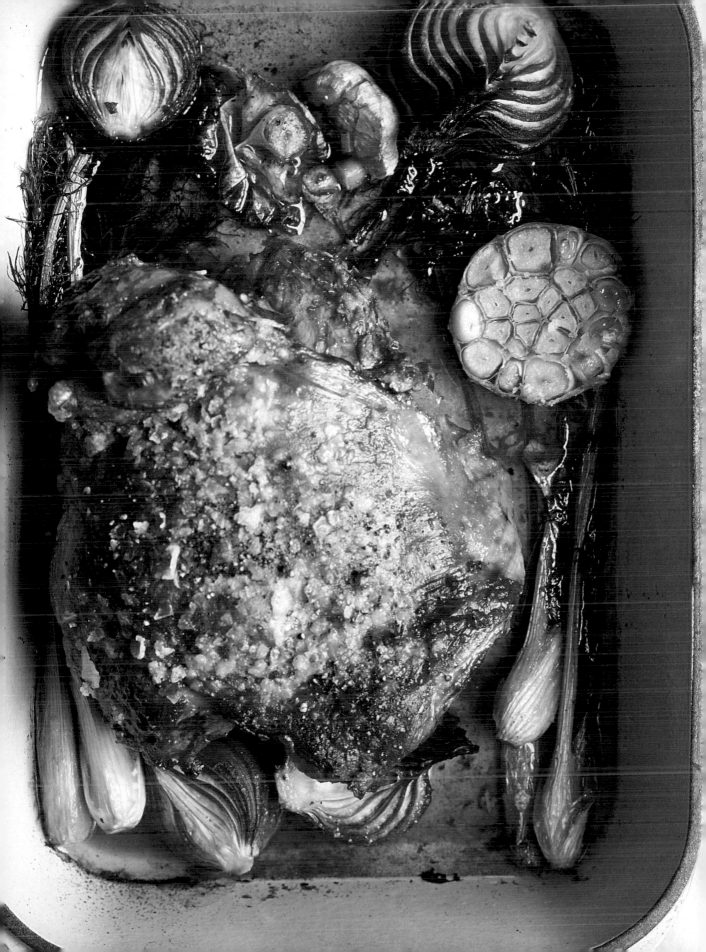

People think that because we live by the sea on the Isle of Wight, we must get marvellous seafood. Well, all we get in season is sea bass, crab and lobster. If you want to catch mackerel you can, but that's the lot from the IOW. But when we do get sea bass it is delicious, and when you catch it yourself it is divine! I fillet the sea bass as it is easier in the long run and nobody eats the heads and tails anyway!

sea bass baked in foil

Adjust all quantities to suit the amount of fish you are cooking.

1 sea bass fillet per person
butter
salt and pepper
limes

1 Put a shallow baking tray into the Roasting Oven to heat up.

2 Tear off a piece of foil big enough to wrap the fish in (you can make individual parcels or one big one). Smear some butter over the bottom of the foil and lay the fish on it, skin side down. Season with salt and pepper and a squeeze of lime juice. Wrap up the fish and remove the now hot baking tray from the oven and lay the fish on to it.

3 Slide the tray on to the third or fourth set of runners in the Roasting Oven and cook the fish for 10–12 minutes or until it is done (I cannot stress enough how awful over-cooked fish is!). Serve with the foil juices and with some green beans.

Conventional Cooking:
Pre-heat the oven to 180°C/350°F/gas 4 and cook as above.

I am a big fan of a mixture of white and brown crab meat, usually mixing it about half white meat to half brown. I must admit I rarely boil my own crab but buy it from my local fishmongers ready picked.

crab tart

serves 6

FOR THE PASTRY:

175g plain flour

100g unsalted butter

salt and pepper

1 egg

FOR THE FILLING:

175ml double cream

large pinch of saffron

olive oil

½ onion or 2 shallots, peeled and finely chopped

5 tomatoes, deseeded, peeled and chopped

1 whole egg

1 egg yolk

175g cooked crab meat, a mix of 75/25 white to brown

salt and pepper

1 To make the pastry, put all the ingredients into a food processor and pulse until they come together to form a ball. Add a little cold water if it is too crumbly. Wrap in cling film and rest in the fridge for at least 30 minutes

2 Bring the pastry to room temperature and roll out. Line a 20.5cm loose-bottomed tart tin with the pastry and set aside in the fridge.

3 Bring the double cream to the boil on the Boiling Plate, then remove from the heat and add the saffron. Leave to infuse for 15 minutes.

4 Heat up about 1 tablespoon olive oil in a frying pan, add the onion or shallots and cook in the Simmering Oven until soft but not coloured. Add the tomatoes and stir well. Season and cook in the Simmering Oven until most of the liquid has evaporated.

5 Beat the eggs together, then stir into the cream. Spread the tomato and onion mix over the bottom of the pastry, then cover with the crab meat. Carefully pour the custard over the crab and set the tart on the Roasting Oven floor with the Cold Plain Shelf on the third or fourth set of runners. Bake for 20–30 minutes or until just set. Serve warm with a side salad.

Conventional Cooking:

Pre-heat the oven to 180°C/350°F/gas 4. When you have lined the tin with the pastry, prick the bottom with a fork and blind-bake the tart shell for 10–12 minutes or until golden. Remove and set aside. Make the filling on the hob as above and fill the cooked pastry shell. Cook the tart at 180°C/350°F/gas 4 for 20–25 minutes.

I like to serve scallops with their coral, but that is personal preference. Freshness is the key and if you can shuck them yourself, so much the better.

pan-fried scallops with chilli and lemon on spaghetti

serves 4

zest and juice of 1 organic lemon

a generous glug of good-quality olive oil, plus a little extra for brushing

1 bird's eye chilli, deseeded and chopped into tiny pieces

1 tbsp chopped flat leaf parsley

1 garlic clove, peeled and crushed

salt and pepper

12 plump shucked scallops, corals on, rinsed and drained

500g spaghetti

1 Mix the lemon zest and juice, olive oil, chopped chilli, parsley, garlic, salt and pepper together in a bowl. Cover with cling film and set aside. (This can be done in advance and placed in the fridge. Take it out of the fridge 30 minutes before using.)

2 Place the Aga grill pan on the floor of the Roasting Oven to heat up, then transfer it to the Simmering Plate. Brush each scallop with a little olive oil and sear in the grill pan. Cook on each side for 1–2 minutes, depending how thick they are. Do not overcrowd the grill pan – you may need to cook them in batches. When cooked, put the scallops on a warmed plate and cover loosely.

3 Meanwhile, bring a large pan of water to a rapid boil and add a good amount of salt to the water. Cook the pasta according to the packet instructions and drain. Pour in the oil and chilli mix. This needs to be kept warm so don't cook the pasta until most of the scallops are cooked.

4 Toss the scallops with the pasta, making sure everything is coated well. Add a little more oil if necessary. Serve with a rocket salad.

Conventional Cooking:
Cook on the hob.

isle of wight kitchen clam bake

serves 6–8

3 tbsp olive oil

2 large onions, peeled and chopped

2 leeks, trimmed and chopped

900g new potatoes

salt and pepper

900g slightly smoked sausage, cut into 2cm slices

24 clams

1kg mussels, cleaned and debearded

900g shell-on prawns

3 lobsters

2 large glasses dry white wine

1 Heat the olive oil in a large stockpot on the Simmering Plate, add the onions and leeks and fry until soft and the onions start to brown.

2 Next, layer on top of the onions in the following order: potatoes, salt and pepper, sausage, clams, mussels, prawns and lobsters. Pour in the wine, cover the pot tightly and cook on the Simmering Plate until steam begins to escape from the lid.

3 Transfer the pot to the Simmering Oven and cook for 25–30 minutes. Test the potatoes to make sure they are cooked and that the clams and mussels are open. Remove the lobsters, crack open the claws and loosen the meat from the shell. Transfer the seafood and vegetables to a warmed dish and top with the lobsters.

4 Strain the broth and add to the seafood and vegetables. Check the seasoning and serve in warmed bowls. Serve with lots of crusty bread to mop up the juices and with a tomato salad and corn-on-the-cob.

Conventional Cooking:

Well, to cook this conventionally, you really need to find a beach, dig a hole and build a fire, but if you can't do that, cook it entirely on the hob using a heat diffuser to ensure a simmer on a low heat.

I do get annoyed by how expensive lobster is. On the east coast of America they treat it almost as a fast food as it is so abundant and that's how I like it – not as something exclusive but to be enjoyed by everyone, either in a sandwich or lovingly thermadored!

lobster rolls

serves 4–6

4 x 1kg live lobsters
grapeseed oil
4–6 bridge rolls
iceberg lettuce, chopped

FOR THE RED PEPPER SAUCE:
250ml olive oil
250ml sunflower oil
2 eggs
½ tsp mustard powder
salt to taste
1 tbsp lemon juice
6 roasted red peppers,
de-seeded, skinned and
finely diced
3 tbsp brandy
1 tbsp pink peppercorns,
crushed

1 Put the live lobsters on a chopping board. Insert the point of a very sharp knife hard into the back of the head and push down to kill the lobster. Cut the lobster in half, straight down the middle of the back. Remove any green intestines.

2 Lay the lobsters in a large roasting tin and drizzle over a little grapeseed oil. Roast them on the second set of runners in the Roasting Oven for 10–15 minutes. Remove them from the oven and allow to cool.

3 To make the sauce, pour the oils into a jug. Whiz the eggs, mustard, salt and lemon juice in a food processor. Pour in the oil little by little until the mixture begins to thicken and it is all used up (like making mayonnaise). Add half the diced pepper and whiz again. Spoon the mixture into a bowl and fold in the remaining diced pepper, brandy and peppercorns. Season to taste and cover with cling film until ready to serve.

4 Take the lobsters out of their shells, de-vein the tails and remove the claw meat in one piece, reserving it to one side. Chop the lobster meat into cubes and combine in a large bowl with 2 tablespoons of the red pepper sauce.

5 Slice each roll almost all the way through and fill with a layer of lettuce, a layer of lobster meat and the claw meat on top. Serve the extra sauce on the side.

Conventional Cooking:
Pre-heat the oven to its highest setting and roast the lobsters or cook them in boiling water.

Corn cooked this way retains all of its sweetness and goodness. This is so easy you will never boil corn again. Do use freshly picked ears if possible. The quantity of corncobs depends on the number of people you are feeding.

baked corn-on-the-cob with roasted garlic butter

2 whole garlic heads
2 tbsp good olive oil
250g butter, at room temperature
salt and pepper
corncobs

1 To make the garlic butter, slice the tops off the garlic heads so the raw cloves are exposed but not separated. Lay the garlic heads on a large piece of foil and drizzle over the olive oil. Tightly wrap the foil around the garlic and place on a baking tray. Pop them into the Roasting Oven for 20 minutes or until the garlic cloves are soft. Set aside to cool.

2 Put the butter, salt and pepper into a bowl. Squeeze the cooled garlic cloves to release the pulp on to the butter and mash it all together. Transfer to a bowl and keep in the fridge until you are ready to serve. This can be made ahead of time and will keep, covered, for up to 2 days in the fridge.

3 Place the grid shelf on the floor of the Roasting Oven. With the husks still on, put the ears of corn on the grid shelf. Cook for about 20–25 minutes. You can stack the ears in the oven but they will take a little longer, and they cook more evenly in a single layer. Serve with the roasted garlic butter and lots of napkins!

Conventional Cooking:
Pre heat the oven to 200°C/400°F/gas 6 and roast the garlic as above. To cook the corn, bring a large pan of water up to a boil, add salt, drop in the corn ears (husks removed) and cook for about 15 minutes.

summer pizza

See page 132 for the basic pizza dough recipe and method. This is my list of suggested spring toppings:

tomato sauce (optional)

fresh tomatoes

buffalo mozzarella cheese

grated courgettes

Parmesan cheese

basil

oregano

I think if you were to ask any of my friends what my slogan is, the answer would be: 'Never knowingly under-catered'. I would have no problem at all should the army ever call me up to cook for them. I am at one with large numbers and my cupboards and fridges are always full to overflowing. It definitely is a genetic thing as all my family are the same. We still shop daily so, with that in mind, I give you the ultimate recipe for when there is nothing in the house! There are a few fruits which I always have in stock – lemons, apples and grapes. A lemon can transform a dish and be used sweet or savoury.

lemon risotto

serves 6

generous knob of butter, about 120g

dash of olive oil

1 onion, peeled and finely chopped

salt and pepper

1 garlic clove, peeled and crushed

300g risotto rice

1 glass of dry martini or white wine

1 litre chicken stock, heated

120g Parmesan cheese, grated, plus more for serving

2–3 tbsp Mascarpone cheese (optional)

zest and juice of 3 organic lemons

handful of basil leaves, torn

1 Put half the butter and a dash of olive oil into a heavy-bottomed frying pan and place it on the floor of the Roasting Oven to heat up. When it is hot, add the onion and put back on to Roasting Oven floor to soften.

2 When the onion is ready, place the pan on the Simmering Plate and add salt and pepper, the garlic and risotto rice and, stirring the entire time, coat the rice in the onion and oil mixture until the rice is translucent. Pour in the dry martini or wine and stir until it is almost all evaporated, then add all the stock, stir and bring to the boil.

3 Transfer the pan to the floor of the Simmering Oven for 20 minutes or the fourth set of runners in the Roasting Oven for 15 minutes. If the risotto is too wet, give it an extra 5 minutes.

4 When the liquid has nearly all been absorbed and the rice is tender but still has a bit of a bite, take the pan out of the oven and stir in the Parmesan and the Mascarpone, if using, the rest of the butter, lemon juice, zest and basil leaves. Check the seasoning and serve with more Parmesan cheese.

Conventional Cooking:
Make in the usual way on the hob, ladling in hot stock and stirring constantly over a medium heat.

Broad beans are so wonderful and their arrival so anticipated that I'm afraid we do indulge in the baby ones at the beginning of the season and eat them straight off the stalk. They never see boiling water! Later on in the season, when they become bigger and tougher, they do need to be cooked and their skins removed. I know this is a bore but it is essential.

broad beans with pasta and ricotta

serves 4

500g tagliolini pasta

olive oil

1 medium onion, peeled and finely chopped

1 garlic clove, peeled and crushed

1 tsp chopped fresh oregano

1 tbspchopped fresh flat leaf parsley

1kg shelled broad beans, blanched and ready to cook (see note)

salt and pepper

extra virgin olive oil, for drizzling

1 organic lemon

60g ricotta cheese

1 Bring a large pot of salted water up to the boil on the Boiling Plate and cook the pasta until it is al dente.

2 While the pasta is cooking, heat 2–3 tablespoons of olive oil in a large frying pan, add the onion and cook on the floor of the Roasting Oven until softened. Add the garlic, herbs and a splash of the pasta water to the pan and gently cook on the Simmering Plate.

3 Drain the pasta, reserving a little of the cooking water, and add the pasta to the onion mix. Toss in the broad beans. Season with salt and pepper.

4 Drizzle over some extra virgin olive oil and gently stir so that the pasta is thoroughly coated, adding a little of the reserved water if it is too dry. Grate the lemon zest over the pasta and crumble in the ricotta cheese. Stir, check the seasoning and serve.

Conventional Cooking:

Cook the pasta in rapidly boiling water over a high heat. Fry the onion in the olive oil over a medium heat and continue as above.

Note:

To prepare the broad beans, shell them, then blanch in rapidly boiling water. Drain the beans, then plunge into ice cold water. Pop each bean out of its pale green skin by pinching with thumb and forefinger.

roasted shallots

serves 4–6

20 shallots
1–2 tbsp olive oil
balsamic or good white wine vinegar
1 tsp sugar
salt and pepper

1 To peel the shallots, put them into a bowl and pour over boiling water. Leave for 10–15 minutes, then peel in the usual way.

2 Put the peeled shallots back into a clean bowl and pour over the olive oil and a splash of balsamic or white wine vinegar. Sprinkle over the sugar and season with salt and pepper.

3 Tip the shallots into a roasting tin and cook in the Roasting Oven for 15–20 minutes or until caramelised and soft. Serve with roasted meats or fish.

Conventional Cooking:
Pre-heat the oven to 180°C/350°F/gas 4 and cook for 20 minutes or until caramelised and soft.

The tops of beets are great for salads. I also roast beets with balsamic vinegar which goes well with their natural sweetness. They are so colourful but do wear gloves when peeling as they will stain hands for days!

balsamic roasted beetroot

serves 4–6

12–16 baby beetroot
olive oil
balsamic vinegar
salt and pepper
½ tbsp fresh thyme
½ tbsp chopped fresh rosemary
12–16 bocconcini (tiny buffalo mozzarella balls)
2 handfuls of rocket

1 Cut the beetroot in half, place on a shallow baking tray and drizzle over some olive oil and balsamic vinegar and season with salt and pepper.

2 Slide the tray on to the second set of runners in the Roasting Oven and roast for about 15–20 minutes or until the beetroot are slightly charred and softish. Remove them from the oven and leave to cool, pouring over any juices left in the bottom of the tin.

3 Put the herbs and bocconcini into a bowl and pour over enough olive oil to just cover them. Cover with cling film.

4 Arrange the rocket on a platter and top with the beetroot and bocconcini balls, tossing everything together lightly. Drizzle over some more balsamic vinegar and season with salt and pepper.

Conventional Cooking:
Pre-heat the oven to 180°C/350°F/gas 4 and cook for 20 minutes as above.

peas with lettuce and prosciutto

serves 4

550g podded fresh peas
1 head of little gem lettuce
4 spring onions, sliced
1 tsp oregano
40g butter
75g sliced prosciutto
salt and pepper

1 Put the peas, lettuce leaves, spring onions, oregano, butter and a splash of water into a saucepan with a lid. Bring it to a rapid simmer on the Simmering Plate.

2 Lay the prosciutto on top, then transfer the pan to the Simmering Oven for 15–20 minutes or until it is tender. Check the seasoning and serve.

Conventional Cooking:

Cook on the hob, then transfer to an oven pre-heated to 180°C/350°F/gas 4 and cook as above.

Now potatoes are best when they come straight out of the ground, so do try and plant a pot of potatoes. My husband is not a big potato lover but he can't get enough of our own home-grown ones. New potatoes do seem to take a lot of cooking for some reason, so if you cook them in the Simmering Oven you may find they take up to 40 minutes.

hot potato salad

serves 4

1kg new potatoes, washed and scraped
1 tbsp red wine vinegar
3 tbsp sunflower oil
1 tsp sweet mustard
salt and pepper
butter
3 streaky rashers of bacon, fried until really crispy, then crumbled or chopped
1 heaped tbsp chopped fresh chives

1 Boil the potatoes in a large pan of water on the Boiling Plate for 3–4 minutes. Drain off all the water, cover with a tight fitting lid and put them on the floor of the Simmering Oven for 30–40 minutes or until tender.

2 To make the dressing, whisk the vinegar, oil, mustard, salt and pepper together and set aside.

3 Remove the potatoes from the oven. If the potatoes are on the large side, halve them. Toss in a knob of butter and the dressing, then stir in the bacon and chives. Serve hot or cold.

Conventional Cooking:
Cook potatoes on the hob in the usual way.

Note:
The trick with potato salad is to dress it while it is hot, then you can serve it hot or cold.

By the end of the summer courgettes do become a little tiresome I admit, but when they are young the best way to eat them is raw with some olive oil and a squeeze of lemon. When I cook them, I like to sauté them in thin ribbons in a bit of butter. Mint and basil go extremely well with them.

sautéed courgettes with basil and mint

serves 4– 6

8–10 medium courgettes
knob of butter
1 handful of basil
1 handful of mint
salt and pepper
Parmesan cheese (optional)

1 Using a potato peeler, peel the courgettes into long ribbons.
2 Melt a knob of butter in a large frying pan on the Simmering Plate. Sauté the courgette ribbons in the butter. When they are almost ready, throw in the basil and mint leaves.
3 Season with salt and pepper and serve. You can shave over some Parmesan if you wish.

Conventional Cooking:
Cook on the hob.

summer fennel slaw

serves 4–6

2 fat bulbs of organic fennel
1 red onion, peeled and thinly sliced
salt and pepper
dash of white wine vinegar
1 heaped tbsp chopped fresh mint
1 heaped tbsp chopped fresh dill
200ml sour cream or crème fraîche

1 Trim and thinly slice the fennel bulbs, reserving the feathery tops.
2 Mix all the ingredients well and adjust seasoning to taste – if it needs to be a little sharper, add some more vinegar. Top with the fennel fronds and serve with chicken, lamb or pork.

sautéed courgettes with basil and mint

I think the best pudding of all in the summer is fresh English strawberries and cream. The most I do is sprinkle over some elderflower cordial or sugar and leave to macerate. I really don't think you can beat this and I serve it all the time. So don't feel you haven't done your bit if you produce a vast bowl of strawberries or raspberries and cream for pudding. All that a summer dinner or lunch really needs is soft fruits, and maybe a ripe cheese. However, for 'proper pudding' lovers, the following are divine!

Raspberries are, to my mind, the king of the berries. The large red raspberries of summer are such a treat that I do nothing to them but serve them with a bowl of thick cream and sugar. Golden raspberries are a delicious treat in the autumn and are wonderful served with duck – well, I like it anyway!

cream cheese lemon roulade

serves 6

200g cream cheese
zest of 2 large organic lemons
juice of 1 large organic lemon
5 eggs separated – you will need
4 yolks and 5 whites
140g golden caster sugar
icing sugar

FOR THE FILLING:
200ml double cream
lemon curd

1 Line a shallow baking tray with Bake-O-Glide.

2 Break up the cream cheese in a bowl with a fork or spoon and stir in the lemon juice and zest until it is smooth.

3 Whisk the egg yolks and caster sugar in an electric mixer for about 5 minutes until they are pale. Stir in the cream cheese mix. Set aside.

4 Whisk the egg whites together until they reach the soft peak stage. Gently fold the pale eggy mix into the egg whites.

5 Spread the roulade mix on to the shallow baking tray and bake on the third set of runners in the Roasting Oven for 8–10 minutes or until it springs back when gently pressed in the centre.

6 While the roulade is baking, lay a clean tea towel over a wire rack and then lay a piece of greaseproof paper over the towel. Sift some icing sugar on to the greaseproof paper.

7 When the roulade is done, remove from the oven and cool in the tin. When it has cooled completely, invert it on to the sugared greaseproof and peel off the Bake-O-Glide.

8 Whip the double cream to soft peaks. Spread the lemon curd over the cake base, then the whipped cream. With the short end of the cake facing you, roll it carefully into a roulade. Wrap in the clean towel and secure the top using clothes pegs or a bulldog clip to hold its shape. Place in the refrigerator. When you are ready to serve, unwrap and dust with icing sugar.

Conventional Cooking:
Pre-heat the oven to 200°C/400°F/gas 6 and proceed as above.

seasonal crumble tart

1 quantity sweet pastry (see page 90)

FOR THE CRUMBLE TOPPING:

175g plain flour

175g ground almonds or hazelnuts to suit the fruit

175g vanilla sugar or muscovado sugar

175g unsalted butter, cut into pieces

spice to suit fruit (eg ½ tsp ground cloves, cinnamon, ground cardamom, etc)

FOR THE NUT FILLING:

60g unsalted butter, softened

60g icing sugar

60g ground almonds or hazelnuts or walnuts

1 whole egg

1 tbsp double cream

FOR THE FRUIT:

approximately 500kg fruit from the following list (if it needs to be stoned and chopped or quartered, then do so):

raspberries

gooseberries, picked over and cooked a little before filling tart

blueberries

cherries (delicious with the almond mix)

apples (alone or with blackberries)

peaches, nectarines and apricots

1 Line a 20.5cm solid bottomed tart tin with sweet pastry. Put the pastry-lined tin in the fridge to chill.

2 To make the crumble topping, put the flour, nuts, sugar, butter and spices (if using) into a large bowl and rub together or pulse in a food processor so that it resembles coarse breadcrumbs.

3 Make the nut filling. Beat all of the ingredients together until thick. Spread over the bottom of the pastry and top with the fruit. Scatter the crumble topping over the fruit.

4 Place the tart on the floor of the Roasting Oven for 30–35 minutes. Check the tart after 15 minutes and slide in the Cold Plain Shelf. The tart should be golden brown and the pastry cooked (there is nothing more off-putting than underdone pastry!). Serve warm with clotted cream or ice cream.

Conventional Cooking:

Pre-heat the oven to 190°C/375°F/gas 5. Blind-bake the pastry case for 10 minutes. Fill and bake in the middle of the oven for 40 minutes or until done, as above.

What could be simpler than an open fruit tart? Use fruits such as peaches, apples, pears, blueberries, apricots and stoned cherries. See the notes below for savoury variations.

summer tarts

serves 4

FOR THE SWEET PASTRY:

300g plain flour

120g golden caster sugar

pinch of salt

120g unsalted butter, cold and cubed

80g polenta

1 egg, beaten

FOR THE FILLING:

65g plain flour

60g caster sugar, plus more for topping

60g unsalted butter, cold and cubed

600g fruit, stoned and chopped if necessary

1 egg yolk, beaten, for egg wash

1 To make the pastry, sift the flour, sugar and salt into the bowl of a food processor, then add the butter and polenta and process for 30 seconds. Add the egg and process again until it forms a ball (you may have to add a little cool water 1 tablespoon at a time if the mixture is dry). Stop immediately, wrap in cling film and rest the pastry in the fridge for a minimum of 30 minutes.

2 To make the filling, put the flour, sugar and butter into the bowl of a food processor and pulse until it is crumbly. Transfer it to a bowl, add the fruit and toss it all together.

3 Roll out the dough into one large circle or 4 medium-sized circles and transfer them to a baking sheet lined with Bake-O-Glide. Pile some of the fruit filling on to the pastry circle, leaving a 5cm border. Carefully fold the border over the fruit, pleating it to make a circle. Brush with the beaten egg and sprinkle over some more sugar.

4 Bake the open pies on the floor of the Roasting Oven with the Cold Plain Shelf on the fourth set of runners for 20–25 minutes or until the pastry crust is golden.

Conventional Cooking:
Pre-heat the oven to 200°C/400°F/gas 6 and bake as above.

Savoury Variations:
Market tarts: use a pizza-type yeast-based dough and top with herbed ricotta cheese and fresh tomatoes, grilled peppers, etc.
Pesto tart: spread pesto on the base of a savoury pastry tart. Make a dressing and toss in cucumbers, chives, avocados, green tomatoes, etc, then pile into the tart case and serve.
Puff pastry: discs of puff pastry can be used for open tarts topped with tomatoes and basil for a stand-by vegetarian main course.
Smoked fish: add oatmeal to a savoury tart dough for a nutty crust and fill with smoked fish.

cherry gratin

serves 6

125ml double cream
50g white breadcrumbs
100g ground almonds
2 eggs
50g golden caster sugar
1 vanilla pod, split
butter, for greasing
500g stoned cherries
demerara sugar, for sprinkling

1 Pour the cream into a food processor bowl and add the breadcrumbs, almonds, eggs and sugar. Scrape in the vanilla seeds from the pod. Blitz until it is combined.

2 Grease an ovenproof gratin dish. Tip the cherries into the bottom of the dish and spoon over the batter. Put the dish on a baking tray and bake in the Roasting Oven for 20–30 minutes or until golden. If it browns too quickly, slide in the Cold Plain Shelf. For 4-oven Aga owners, bake the gratin in the Baking Oven for 30–35 minutes.

3 Remove the gratin from the oven and sprinkle with the demerara sugar. Serve with clotted cream or ice cream.

Conventional Cooking:
Pre-heat the oven to 200°C/400°F/gas 6 and bake as above.

summer victoria sponge

serves 4–6

175g self-raising flour
175g soft unsalted butter
175g caster sugar
1 tsp vanilla extract
3 large organic eggs
1 rounded tsp baking powder

FOR THE FILLING:
whipped cream
raspberries
icing sugar

1 Line two 20cm loose-bottomed cake tins with Bake-O-Glide.

2 Put all the cake ingredients into the bowl of an electric mixer. Using the beater attachment, beat until combined. Divide the cake mix between the prepared cake tins.

3 Place the grid shelf on the floor of the Roasting Oven and place the cake tins to the right on the grid shelf. Slide the Cold Plain Shelf on to the third set of runners and bake the cakes for 20 minutes or until golden on top, gently coming away from the sides and springing back when lightly pressed on top. For 4-oven Aga owners, cook the cakes on the fourth set of runners in the Baking Oven and use the plain shelf only if browning too quickly.

4 Stand the cake tins on a wire rack for a minute, then remove them from the tin and cool on the wire rack.

5 When the cakes are cool, whip the cream to soft peaks and spread on to one cake, then top with the raspberries and the second cake. Dust the top with icing sugar.

Conventional Cooking:
Pre-heat the oven to 170°C/325°F/gas 3 and bake for 30–35 minutes.

Note:
The quality of the eggs used will affect the cake's flavour and texture. I like to use 2-day-old organic free-range eggs.

blueberry and peach cake

serves 4–6

425g self-raising flour
1 tsp baking powder
240g butter, soft
200g golden caster sugar
3 eggs
1 tsp vanilla extract
350g chopped peaches
150g blueberries

1 Line a 34.5 x 24cm traybake tin with Bake-O-Glide.

2 Put the flour, baking powder, butter, sugar, eggs and vanilla extract into a food processor with a paddle attachment and mix to a smooth dough.

3 Take out one-third of the dough and press the rest into the prepared tin. The dough will be sticky so you may want to press it in with your hand inside a freezer bag or wet your fingers with cold water. Spread the fruit on top and scatter with clumps of the reserved dough.

4 Slide the tin on to the fourth set of runners in the Roasting Oven and bake for about 20–30 minutes or until done. If it browns too quickly, slide in the Cold Plain Shelf. For 4-oven Aga owners, bake on the third set of runners in the Baking Oven for about 30 minutes. Allow the cake to cool in the tin.

Conventional Cooking:
Pre-heat the oven to 180°C/350°F/gas 4 and bake for about 50 minutes.

focaccia al formaggio

makes 1 large loaf

30g yeast
550ml water, plus more if needed
1kg strong flour
30g sea salt, plus extra for sprinkling
120ml olive oil, plus extra for greasing
550g Taleggio cheese, cut into cubes

1 Crumble the yeast into the water and mix until smooth. Put the flour and sea salt into the bowl of a food processor with a dough hook. Start the motor and slowly pour in the yeast, then the oil. Knead until elastic and smooth. Don't be alarmed if it looks sloppy to begin with as it will pull together.

2 Lightly grease a large bowl with olive oil and turn out the dough into it. Cover with a damp tea towel and place it next to the Aga for about an hour or until it has doubled in size.

3 When the bread has had its first proving, knock it back by punching the air out and divide into two unequal pieces – one-third and two-thirds.

4 Line a large roasting tin with Bake-O-Glide. Roll the two pieces of dough out and use the larger one to line the roasting tin. Cover with the cheese, then place the remaining dough on top. Sprinkle with sea salt and push your fingers into it for a dimpled effect. Leave next to the Aga for its second proving.

5 When the dough has doubled in size, place the tin on the floor of the Roasting Oven for 20–25 minutes. If it browns too quickly, insert the Cold Plain Shelf on the second set of runners. Cool in the tin for a few minutes, then remove the Bake-O-Glide and move to a wire rack. Eat warm.

Conventional Cooking:
Pre-heat the oven to 220°C/425°F/gas 7 and continue as above. If it browns too quickly, turn the oven down.

Cherries are so versatile in that they can be eaten raw, preserved or in lots of lovely sweet or savoury combinations. Nothing cheers up a grey winter day like cherries steeped in brandy (see page 100) spooned over home-made vanilla ice cream!

cherry focaccia bread

makes 1 large loaf

30g yeast

550ml warm water, plus more if needed

1kg strong flour

200g golden caster sugar

pinch sea salt

120ml light olive oil, plus extra for dribbling

1.5kg cherries, stoned

1 Crumble the yeast into the water and mix until smooth. Put the flour, half of the sugar and the salt into the bowl of a food processor with the dough hook in place. Start the motor and slowly pour in the yeast, then the olive oil. Knead until it becomes smooth and elastic. Don't be alarmed if it looks sloppy to begin with as it will pull together.

2 Lightly grease a large bowl and turn out the focaccia dough into it. Cover with a damp tea towel and place it next to the Aga for about an hour or until it has doubled in size.

3 When the bread has had its first proving, knock it back by punching the air out. Line a large roasting tin with a large piece of Bake-O-Glide and shape the dough into the tin, stretching it to fit. Scatter over the cherries and using your fingers, press them into the dough, giving it a dimpled effect. Leave the tin next to the Aga again for its second proving and when it has doubled in size, drizzle over a little olive oil and the remaining sugar.

4 Place the tin on the floor of the Roasting Oven and bake the bread for 20–25 minutes. If it browns too quickly, insert the Cold Plain Shelf on the second set of runners.

5 Cool in the tin for a few minutes, then remove the Bake-O-Glide and move to a wire rack to finish cooling.

Conventional Cooking:
Pre-heat the oven to 220°C/425°F/gas 7 and continue as above. If it browns too quickly, turn the oven down.

This is a basic recipe for chutney. You can adjust all the fruit and veg to the season or the glut! Remember to stone fruits that need it and skin things like pumpkins and squashes or anything with a very tough skin. I find that some of the best chutneys I've ever made cannot be repeated because they are made with whatever was around at the time and I didn't write it down, so do make a note of what is in yours and label the jars well. Sometimes it is a good idea to pep up the chutney with a teaspoon of dried chilli flakes or even a minced fresh chilli, depending on how much heat you like.

It is always much better to stand a chutney for at least 4 weeks before eating as it gives it time to let the flavours develop. All the same rules apply to the preparation of jars and seals etc as they do in jam making (see page 14).

basic chutney

makes about 10 jars

BASIC BASE FOR CHUTNEY:

1kg vegetables such as courgettes

1kg acid fruit, such as tomatoes or plums

1kg apples or pears, peeled

500g onions, peeled

500g sultanas or raisins

500g brown sugar

700ml cider vinegar

150ml water

about 1 tsp sea salt

FOR THE SPICE BAG:

6 allspice berries

blade of mace

1 tsp black peppercorns

1 tsp coriander seeds

about 4cm fresh ginger, sliced

½ tsp cloves

and/or anything else you want to put into the bag

1 To make the spice bag, you will need a largish square piece of muslin and some butcher's string. Spread out the muslin and put all the spices into the middle, then gather up the corners and tie tightly with butcher's string.

2 All the vegetables should be deseeded and chopped. With vegetables like pumpkins, the skin should be removed. Tomatoes should be skinned and deseeded, but fruit likes plums can just be stoned and chopped.

3 Put all the ingredients into a large heavy-bottomed stainless steel pan (do not use copper or aluminium for this) and heat slowly on the Simmering Plate until the sugar dissolves.

4 Move to the Boiling Plate and boil for 3–4 minutes, then transfer to the Simmering Oven for 2–3 hours or until it is very thick and a spoon leaves behind a clean trail. Ladle into sterilised jars (see page 14), seal and label. Chutneys should be left to age for a minimum of 1 month before using.

Conventional Cooking:
Cook over a medium heat and bring slowly to the boil. Turn down the heat and gently simmer for about 2 hours or until the chutney is thick, as above.

tomato and chilli chutney

makes 1½–2kg

2kg tomatoes, red and green

500g onions, peeled and chopped

1kg cooking apples, cored and chopped

500g sultanas

3 hot small chillies, finely chopped

500g sugar

750ml cider vinegar, made up to 1 litre with water

1 tsp sea salt

FOR THE SPICE BAG:

12 black peppercorns

1 tsp coriander seeds

3 garlic cloves, peeled and cracked

1 Tie up the black peppercorns, coriander seeds and garlic cloves in a clean piece of muslin.

2 Skin the tomatoes by cutting a cross at the base of each one and standing in boiling water for 3–5 minutes. Peel off the skin and chop the flesh roughly.

3 Put all the ingredients into a large preserving pan which will fit into the Simmering Oven. Bring the mixture up to the boil on the Simmering Plate, then move to the Boiling Plate but do not allow it to catch on the bottom. Stir to dissolve the sugar.

4 Move to the Simmering Oven for 3–4 hours or until the chutney is thick and reduced and when a wooden spoon is dragged through it leaves a clean trail.

5 Ladle the chutney into sterilised jars (see page 14) and seal. Label and keep in a dark place for 1 month or longer before eating.

Conventional Cooking:
Cook on the hob.

This is my paternal grandmother's recipe, called Bread and Butter Pickles not because it has either in the recipe, but because she used to eat them with bread and butter. They are also great with hamburgers, sandwiches or straight out of the jar!

bread and butter pickles

makes about 4 jars

25 medium cucumbers, thinly sliced

12 small onions, peeled and thinly sliced

60g sea salt

550g caster sugar

2 tsp turmeric

2 tsp capers (optional)

2 tsp mustard seeds

2 tsp celery seeds

1 litre white distilled vinegar, mixed with 200ml water

1 Put the cucumbers and onions in iced water with the salt for 3 hours.

2 Put the rest of the ingredients into a large stainless steel pan and bring to the boil on the Boiling Plate.

3 Drain the cucumbers and onions. Remove the pan from the heat and add the cucumbers and onions. Stir for 2 minutes and then ladle into sterilised jars. Seal and label. Stand in a dark place for one month before eating.

Conventional Cooking:
Cook on the hob.

red onion confit

makes 1 jar

2 tbsp olive oil

1 tbsp butter

6 red onions, peeled and thinly sliced

1 tsp caster sugar

salt and pepper

1 tsp mixed spices

1 Put the oil and butter into a saucepan, add the onions and cook very gently on the Simmering Plate until the butter has melted. Add the sugar, salt, pepper and spices and stir well.

2 Transfer the pan to the Simmering Oven and cook for about 45 minutes or until the onions are soft and golden.

3 Spoon into a sterilised jar (see page 14) and cool. Store in the fridge for up to a week. Serve with pâté and cold meats.

Conventional Cooking:
Cook the onion confit over a medium heat on the hob. Simmer over a low heat until the onions are thick and soft.

mint sauce

large bunch of fresh mint leaves, washed, spun or shaken dry, and picked over

2 tbsp golden caster sugar

2 tbsp hot water

2 tbsp vinegar

1 Chop the mint finely and mix with the sugar.

2 Pour the hot water over and stir until the sugar has dissolved. Add the vinegar and leave to infuse for a few hours. Serve with lamb.

Note:
To preserve mint when you have a glut of it, chop up clean mint leaves, mix with golden syrup and store in the fridge. All you have to do when you want to make the sauce above is add hot water and vinegar.

deluxe mint sauce

55g butter

1 large onion, peeled and chopped

2 tbsp chopped fresh mint

½ tsp caster sugar

salt and pepper

1 Melt the butter in a pan on the Simmering Plate. Add the onion and sweat until very soft but not coloured at all.

2 Add the mint, sugar and salt and pepper. Whiz up in a food processor until smooth. Keep warm and serve with lamb.

Conventional Cooking:
Cook on the hob

I know tomatoes are technically a fruit but they are my passion and I eat them every day – my ideal lunch is tomatoes with salt and olive oil and some bread. There are so many different varieties that we are spoilt for choice but nothing beats a cherry tom straight off the bush. My earliest memory of my great-aunt's farm is taking a salt cellar out to the garden and just munching away (I think I was about 4). To skin tomatoes, make a small cross-shaped incision on the bottom, then pop them in a bowl of boiling water for a few minutes and, wearing rubber gloves, peel off the skin. You can do this with shallots and peaches too. Please don't refrigerate your tomatoes – keep them at room temperature. Good ones are heavy for their size. Ripe tomatoes only keep for a few days.

tomato ketchup

makes about 1 litre

30ml olive oil

1 large onion, peeled and finely chopped

1 garlic clove, peeled

1 tsp chopped fresh thyme

950g tomatoes, peeled and chopped

120g sugar

120ml cider vinegar

3 tbsp tomato paste

½ tsp mustard powder

½ tsp cayenne pepper

½ tsp allspice

salt

1 Heat the oil in a large stainless steel saucepan. Add the onions, and garlic and cook until soft.

2 Put the thyme into a muslin wrap and toss into the pan with everything else. Bring to the boil on the Boiling Plate, then simmer, covered, for 30–40 minutes in the Simmering Oven until the mixture starts to thicken.

3 Discard the muslin wrap. Purée the ketchup a food processor and strain through a medium nylon sieve. Return the ketchup to the pan and simmer, uncovered, for another 30–40 minutes in the Simmering Oven to thicken. When it has reached the desired thickness, remove from the oven.

4 Sieve the ketchup through a fine stainless steel sieve, then ladle into sterilised bottles and seal tightly. Keep in the refrigerator for up to 3 months.

Conventional Cooking:
Cook on the hob.

This must be made with Sicilian lemons! First you need to make preserved lemons. You will need a sterilised, wide-mouthed jar with a lid for this. The relish is great served with fish.

sicilian lemon relish

FOR THE PRESERVED LEMONS:

Sicilian lemons – enough to fill the jar

lots of sea salt

FOR THE RELISH:

1 preserved lemon

1 red onion, peeled and chopped pepper

1 tbsp flat leaf parsley

2 tbsp olive oil

8–10 green olives, stored in olive oil, stoned

1 Wash the lemons. Make two deep cuts into each lemon almost all the way through but with their bases still intact so that they are divided into quarters but they remain intact. Do this over a plate to catch the juice.

2 Fill all the cuts with salt. Do this over the plate to catch any juice. Sprinkle a layer of salt into the jar and add some lemons, layering with salt as you go. Do this until the jar is packed with lemons. Pour in any juices on the plate and finish with a layer of salt.

3 Cover the jars and leave in a dark room for a few days. The lemons should be submerged in juice after a few days, if not add more lemon juice. The preserved lemons will be ready to use in four weeks. Keep them in the refrigerator.

4 To make the relish, put the lemon, onion, pepper, parsley, olive oil and olives into a food processor. Pulse until the ingredients are finely chopped but with a little texture. Check for seasoning and add more olive oil if the relish is too stiff – you want a slack mixture.

Make these wonderful preserved fruits when they are in season – most will be ready for Christmas. For each 500g of fruit you will need 220ml water and 220g unrefined sugar.

fruits steeped in liqueurs

Peaches in brandy

Strawberries in white rum

Oranges in Cointreau

Plums in brandy

Nectarines in Amaretto

Cherries in Kirsch

Apricots in Amaretto

Cherries in brandy

Damsons in port

Raspberries in port

1 First choose perfect ripe fruit. Wash it and wipe. In the case of fuzzy fruits such as peaches and apricots, rub off the fuzz with a clean tea towel.

2 Weigh the fruit and measure out the sugar and water. Put the sugar and water into a saucepan and bring to the boil on the Boiling Plate for 2–3 minutes. Add the fruit to the stock syrup and return to the boil and cook for 4–5 minutes. (Berries do not have to be added to the syrup and boiled – just pack them into jars and pour in the syrup and alcohol.)

3 Pack the fruit into sterilised wide-mouthed jars using a slotted spoon and pour in the hot stock syrup so the jar is half full. Top up with chosen liqueur to fill the jars within 3cm of the top. Seal and store in a dark place for a minimum of two months.

sicilian lemon relish

lemon verbena tisane

a few tender sprigs of lemon verbena

freshly boiled mineral water

sugar or lemon slices

1 Pack the leaves into a teapot and pour over the freshly boiled water.

2 Leave to infuse for a few minutes, then pour into cups. Sweeten with sugar if desired or serve with a slice of lemon.

Note:

Use a glass teapot to make this, as the colour is glorious! You can also make tisanes out of lots of other herbs – try rosemary, thyme, mint or camomile flower heads. Freshly boiled mineral water may sound extravagant but it's worth using this with such tender leaves.

green apple tea

serves 4

1 organic Granny Smith apple

650ml freshly boiled mineral water

1 Core the apple and slice. Put the slices into a teapot or cafetière and pour over the water.

2 Infuse for 10 minutes. Serve.

Note:

Flower infusions can be made in the same way, and can be served with a sugar swizzle stick. Try using borage or jasmine flowers, or elderflower. Herbs such as mint, rosemary or lavender can also be used.

vin d'orange

makes about 1 litre

250ml vodka

the thin peels of 2 organic oranges

4 walnut leaves or 5 star anise

105g unrefined golden caster sugar

1 bottle of red wine, such as Zinfandel

lots of ice and lemon zest, to serve

1 Combine the vodka, orange peels and star anise or walnut leaves in a kilner jar and stand for 2 weeks, shaking the jar daily or whenever you think about it!

2 Strain the liquid into another large jar. Add the sugar and wine and shake or stir until the sugar has dissolved. Stand for 24 hours.

3 Pour the drink over lots of ice and serve with a slice of lemon zest.

green apple tea and lemon verbena tisane

elderflower cordial

makes 2 litres

1.7 litres still mineral water

1.8kg golden caster sugar

20 perfect elderflower heads

zest and juice of 4 organic
lemons

85g citric acid (available from
chemists)

1 Boil the water in a stainless steel pan on the Boiling Plate, remove from the heat and stir in the sugar. Cover with a clean tea towel and leave to cool.

2 When the water is cool, stir in the elderflower heads, lemon juice and zest and citric acid. Cover with a clean tea towel and leave for 4–5 days in a cool dark area.

3 Strain into sterilised bottles and seal. Leave for 1 month before using. Dilute to taste with sparkling or still mineral water and serve with ice. I also pour cordial over strawberries and raspberries before serving.

Conventional Cooking:
Boil the water on the hob.

lemon verbena cordial

makes 1 litre

1.7 litres still mineral water

1.5kg golden caster sugar

4 good handfuls of lemon
verbena leaves

80g citric acid (available from
chemists)

zest and juice of 4 organic
lemons

1 Boil the water in a stainless steel pan on the Boiling Plate, remove from the heat and stir in the sugar. Cover with a clean tea towel and leave to cool.

2 When the water is cool, take the lemon verbena leaves and crush them slightly with your hands. Stir them into the water along with the lemon juice and zest and citric acid. Cover with a clean tea towel and leave for 2–3 days in a cool dark area.

3 Strain into sterilised bottles and seal. You can use the cordial straight away. Store opened bottles in the fridge. Dilute to taste with sparkling or still mineral water and serve with ice.

Conventional Cooking:
Boil the water on the hob.

rose petal confiture

makes 2 pots of jam

250g highly perfumed red rose petals (no insects please!)
500g jam sugar
75ml water
juice of 1 lemon
3 tbsp rose water

1 Start to make this jam the day before. Cut off the white base of the rose petal and cut the petals very thinly with a sharp knife. Put them into a bowl and sprinkle about a tablespoon of the sugar over them. Cover with cling film and leave for 24 hours.

2 The next day, bring the rose petals, water, lemon juice and the rest of the sugar to the boil in a preserving pan on the Boiling Plate and boil for about 20 minutes, or boil on the Roasting Oven floor (this may take a little longer) until you reach a set.

3 To test for a set, place a saucer in the freezer while the jam is boiling. After 20 minutes of rapid boiling, take the jam off the heat and drop a spoonful on to the cold saucer. Push the jam with your finger – if it wrinkles it is ready; if not boil for a further 5 minutes or until it reaches setting point. The jam should look like a thick syrup.

4 When it is ready, add the rose water and pour the jam into sterilised jam jars. Seal with a lid and cool.

Conventional Cooking:
Cook in the usual way on the hob.

Note:
This is worth making in June so that you can enjoy the scent of the summer at a deep winter tea party. Use jam sugar as this has added pectin and acid.

autumn

what's in season?

September

Fruits
Apples
Autumn raspberries
Blackberries
Bullace (wild food)
Cape gooseberries
  (hot house)
Crab apples
Damsons
Elderberries (wild)
Figs (LSEA)
Greengages
Hips (wild)
Medlars (wild)
Mulberries (LSEA)
Plums
Quinces
Pears

Vegetables
Borlotti beans
Onions (LSEA)
Potatoes (main
  crop, see note
  on page 179)
Samphire
Turnips
Wild mushrooms

Herbs
Basil
Chives
Coriander
Dill
Fennel
Horseradish
Mint
Rosemary
Sage
Thyme

Nuts
Cobnuts
Chestnuts
Hazelnuts
Wet walnuts

Meat
Grouse
Guinea fowl
  (available all year)
Hare
Mutton
Partridge
Pigeon
Quail
Rabbit
Snipe

Venison
Wild boar
Wild duck

Fish and seafood
Cod
Crab
Dublin Bay prawns
Haddock
Halibut
John Dory
Lemon sole
Monkfish
Oysters
Plaice
Scallops
Skate
Wild brown trout
Wild salmon

October

Fruit
Apples
Autumn raspberries
Bullace (wild food)
Cape gooseberries
  (hot house)
Crab apples
Damsons
Elderberries (wild)
Figs (LSEA)
Greengages
Hips (wild)
Medlars (wild)
Mulberries (LSEA)
Pears
Plums
Quinces
Rhubarb (forced)
Sloes (after first frost)

Vegetables
Beetroot
Borlotti beans
Broccoli
Cabbage
Cardoons
Carrots
Cauliflower
Celeriac
Celery
Chard
Fennel
Garlic (new)
Globe artichokes
Jerusalem artichokes
  (late October)
Onions (new and
  stored)

Potatoes (main
  crop, see note
  on page 179)
Pumpkins and
  squashes
Radicchio (and
  the start of
  some chicories)
Radishes
Shallots (new
  and stored)
Spinach
Swedes
Turnips
Wild mushrooms

Nuts and berries
Chestnuts
Cobnuts (gone by
  the middle to end
  of October)
Juniper berries
Wet walnuts

Meat
Grouse
Guinea fowl
Hare
Mutton
Partridge
Pigeon
Pork
Quail
Rabbit
Snipe
Venison
Wild boar
Wild duck
Wild goose
Woodcock

Fish and seafood
Bream
Cod
Crab
Haddock
Halibut
John Dory
Lemon sole
Monkfish
Oysters
Plaice
Red mullet
Scallops
Skate
Wild brown trout
Wild salmon

Herbs
Basil
Rosemary
Sage
Thyme

Dairy
Vacherin Mont d'Or
  cheese

November

Fruit
Apples
Autumn raspberries
Cape gooseberries
  (hot house
  September–
  December)
Crab apples
Damsons
Figs (LSEA)
Greengages
Medlars (wild)
Mulberries (LSEA)
Pears
Plums
Pomegranates
Quinces
Rhubarb (forced)
Sloes (after first frost)

Vegetables
Beetroot
Broccoli
Brussels sprouts
Cauliflower
Cabbage
Cardoons
Carrots
Celeriac
Celery
Chard
Chicory
Endive
Fennel
Garlic (new)
Globe artichokes
Jerusalem artichokes
Leeks
Onions (new and
  stored)
Parsnips
Potatoes (main crop,
  see note on page
  179)
Pumpkins and
  squashes
Radicchio
Radishes
Salsify

Shallots (new
  and stored)
Spinach
Swedes
Tomatoes (hot
  house)
Turnips
Wild mushrooms

Herbs
Basil
Rosemary
Sage
Thyme

Nuts
Chestnuts

Meat
Grouse
Guinea fowl
Hare
Mutton
Partridge
Pigeon
Pork
Quail
Rabbit
Snipe
Venison
Wild boar
Wild duck
Wild goose
Woodcock

Fish and seafood
Brown crab
Cod
Crab
Lobster
Mackerel
Mussels
Oysters
Prawns
Scallops
Sea bass
Squid
Wild brown trout
Wild salmon

Dairy
Truffle cheese
  (Formaggio di
  Tartufo)
Vacherin Mont d'Or
  cheese

Note
LSEA = late
  summer/early
  autumn

autumn recipes

Soups and Starters
Hot Prawn Chowder with Rice
Chicken Noodle Soup
Butternut Squash and Ginger Soup
Bread and Bean Soup
Soda Bread
Truffled Scrambled Eggs on Sourdough
   Toast
Fig and Cobnut Salad
Chicken Liver Pâté

Main Courses/Meat
Sausages with Apples and Smoked
   Applewood Cheese
Apple Sauce
Sticky Sausages with Roasted Garlic Mash
Shoulder of Pork with Chilli and Sage
Bacon, Chestnut and Wild Mushroom
   Penne
Roasted Pheasant with Quince Cheese
Pomegranate and Pheasant Salad
Pan-fried Pigeon Breasts with Maltaise
   Sauce
Roast Partridge with Apples and Pears
Shredded Chicken with Polenta and
   Wild Mushrooms
Roast Duck with Pumpkin Sage Mash

Main Courses/Fish
Skate Wings with Porcini Powder
Pancetta-wrapped Prawns

Main Courses/Vegetarian
Autumn Pizza
Pumpkin Risotto
Wild Mushroom Risotto with Crispy
   Sage Leaves

Accompaniments
Roasted Pumpkin
Portobello Mushrooms with Parsley
   and Garlic

Desserts and Baking
Damsons in Distress
Poached Quinces in Pudding Wine
Baked Apples with Cinnamon Crumble
   Topping
Pear and Orange Crunch
Caramel Apples
Apple Custard
Roasted Plums with Taleggio Cheese
Autumn Berry Cobbler
Crumble Toppings
Apple Cake

Preserves
Oven-made Raspberry and Blackberry Jam
Apple Butter
Damson Cheese
Quince Cheese

SOUPS AND STARTERS

hot prawn chowder with rice

serves 6–8

180g unsalted butter

2 onions, peeled and finely chopped

4 stalks of celery, peeled and finely chopped

1 red bird's eye chilli, deseeded and finely chopped (or more if you like it hot)

salt and pepper

75g flour

750ml chicken stock

300g rice

1.5kg fresh king prawns, de-veined and shelled

250ml double cream

zest of 2 limes, plus the juice of 3

chopped fresh flat leaf parsley

1 Melt the butter in a large deep pan on the Simmering Plate, add the onion and gently soften until translucent but not coloured. Add the celery, chilli, salt and pepper and cook for 8–10 minutes on the Simmering Plate. Do not let anything get too brown. Add the flour, stir and cook for 5 minutes.

2 Pour in the stock little by little, stirring all the time. Bring up to a boil and then simmer for another 15–20 minutes or until it starts to thicken slightly. (Usually I would say to do this in the Simmering Oven but as this is such a meal in itself, do it on the Simmering Plate.)

3 Meanwhile, cook the rice in a pan of water. Bring to the boil on the Boiling Plate, stir once, cover with a lid and place on the floor of the Simmering Oven for 18–20 minutes, or until cooked.

4 Add the prawns, cooked rice, cream, lime zest and juice, and parsley to the onions. Gently heat through for a few minutes on the Simmering Plate. Season to taste and serve with lots of crusty bread.

Conventional Cooking:
Cook on the hob.

chicken noodle soup

serves 6

1.5–2kg organic chicken

1 bouquet garni made up of rosemary, sage, thyme and flat leaf parsley

3 carrots, washed and scrubbed

2 whole onions, peeled

2 stalks celery, peeled

2 litres chicken stock

salt and pepper

250g dried wide egg noodles

flat leaf parsley, to serve

1 Put the chicken into a large pot and add the bouquet garni, carrots, onions and celery. Cover this with the chicken stock and about 500ml water. Season with salt and pepper.

2 Bring up to the boil on the Boiling Plate for 10 minutes, then transfer to the Simmering Oven for 2–3 hours.

3 When the soup is cooked and the meat is coming away from the bones, remove it with the bouquet garni and the vegetables. Take the meat off the bones and shred it, discarding the skin and bones. Discard the onions but chop up the carrots and celery. Put the vegetables back into the stock, add the noodles and cook on the Simmering or Boiling Plate for as long as the packet says (usually about 8 minutes).

4 Add the shredded chicken and some more chopped parsley. Check the seasoning and serve.

Conventional Cooking:
Cook the whole recipe on the hob, simmering for 1–2 hours.

hot prawn chowder with rice

butternut squash and ginger soup

serves 6

1.5kg butternut squash

3 tbsp olive oil

1 leek, trimmed and sliced thinly

2 garlic cloves, peeled and crushed

1 parsnip, peeled and chopped

6cm piece of fresh ginger, grated, or more to taste

750ml good vegetable or chicken stock

salt and pepper

FOR THE CROUTONS

1 loaf stale ciabatta bread, cut into bite-sized pieces

1 tbsp olive oil

Parmesan curls (see note)

1 Cut the butternut squash in half. Remove the seeds and any fibres, then slice the halves into quarters. Place in a roasting tin. Brush each quarter with a teaspoon of olive oil and sprinkle over some salt and pepper. Roast in the Roasting Oven for about 20 minutes or until soft and slightly charred around the edges. Set aside to cool, then scrape away the squash flesh from the skin and reserve.

2 While the squash is cooking, heat the remaining olive oil in a deep pan on the Simmering Plate. Add the leek and garlic and cook gently until soft. Add the parsnip and ginger and cook for 3–5 minutes. Pour in the stock, bring to the boil, then transfer to the Simmering Oven for 20–25 minutes or until the parsnips are tender.

3 Meanwhile, make the croutons. Toss the pieces of bread in a bowl with the olive oil, making sure they are well coated. Spread on a baking tray and bake in the Roasting or Baking Oven for 8–10 minutes, or until golden. Watch them carefully as they can burn very easily. Leave to cool on a plate lined with kitchen towel.

4 When the soup is ready, tip in the roasted butternut squash and check the seasoning, adding salt and pepper as needed. Pour into a food processor and purée the soup, then return to the pan and warm through. Serve with the croutons and garnish each serving with 2–3 Parmesan curls.

Conventional Cooking:
Pre-heat the oven to 200°C/400°F/gas 6 and roast the squash as above. Make the rest of the soup on the hob. Bake the croutons at 190°C/375°F/gas 5 for 8–10 minutes.

Note:
To make the Parmesan curls, take a hunk of Parmesan cheese and shave the curls off using a potato peeler.

bread and bean soup

serves 6–8

500g borlotti beans, soaked overnight

olive oil

2 onions, peeled and chopped

4 stalks celery, chopped

1 tbsp chopped fresh rosemary

1 tbsp chopped fresh sage

bay leaf

3 fat garlic cloves, peeled

400g piece of pancetta or smoked belly pork

400g tin tomatoes

550g cavolo nero or kale, chopped, with tough centre rib removed

1 litre chicken stock

pepper

1 loaf stale ciabatta bread

Parmesan cheese

1 Drain the beans from their soaking water. Tip into a large casserole and cover with cold water. Bring to the boil on the Boiling Plate for 10 minutes, then transfer to the Simmering Oven for 35 minutes. Strain the beans, reserving the cooking liquid.

2 Heat some olive oil in a large saucepan and gently fry the onions and celery until they are soft but not coloured. Add the herbs, garlic, pancetta, tomatoes, cavolo nero, beans and stock. Season with some pepper. The pancetta may be quite salty so hold off on the salt until the end. Bring to the boil on the Boiling Plate for 5 minutes, then transfer to the Simmering Oven for 1 hour.

3 Tear up the bread into bite-sized pieces, add to the soup and continue to cook for another 20 minutes or so. You may need to add a little of the drained bean water if the liquid level has gone down.

4 When you are ready to serve, check the seasoning and shave over lots of Parmesan cheese. You can cut up the pancetta and give everyone a piece.

Conventional Cooking:
Cook on the hob.

Buttermilk is the milk left after butter has been taken from the churn. It is ideal for making cakes and scones as it is lighter than fresh milk and has a natural effervescent quality.

soda bread

makes 1 loaf

450g plain white flour

1 tsp baking soda

1 tsp cream of tartar

1 tsp salt

350ml buttermilk

1 Sieve the flour, baking soda, cream of tartar and salt into a large bowl. Make a well in the centre of the flour and pour in the buttermilk. Mix it together by hand, then knead a couple of times on a piece of Bake-O-Glide. Shape into a ball and cut a cross on the top.

2 Put the Bake-O-Glide with the soda bread on it on to the floor of the Roasting Oven and bake for 15 minutes. Slide in the Cold Plain Shelf and bake for a further 10 minutes, or until the bread sounds hollow when tapped underneath.

3 Cool on a cooling rack. Serve warm with butter. This bread is great served with cheese and soups.

Conventional Cooking:
Pre-heat the oven to 200°C/400°F/gas 6 and cook the bread on a heated baking tray for 30–35 minutes or until it sounds hollow when tapped.

Truffles are a part of every food lover's autumn ritual. If you have never tasted one, treat yourself and start with this recipe. It is so simple but will give you a lot of satisfaction and will gently ease you into the world of truffles! Brush the truffle lightly with a soft brush or damp cloth and scrape away any spots of dirt with a sharp knife.

Read this recipe thoroughly before you start as, although it is very easy, you need to prepare the eggs well in advance. You will need help making this – a person to toast the bread so that it is just right, leaving you free to make the eggs. I know this seems a lot of fuss for a few scrambled eggs but if you have spent a fortune on the truffle, everything else should be perfect!

truffled scrambled eggs on sourdough toast

serves 6–8

1 black truffle, about 30g

12 organic eggs, as fresh as possible

1 loaf sourdough bread

salt

250ml whipping cream

75g unsalted butter, plus more for buttering the toast

1 You will need a lidded container large enough to hold all the eggs and the truffle. Carefully lay the eggs in the container, put the truffle in the middle of them and close the lid. Store the eggs in this way for at least 3 days. (You can use more eggs if you wish.)

2 Toast and butter the bread to coincide with the eggs being ready.

3 Crack the eggs into a glass bowl. Cut the truffle into small dice and add half to the eggs. Add a little salt and cream and beat the eggs gently.

4 Melt half the butter in a large non-stick pan on the Simmering Plate and pour in the eggs. Stir the eggs constantly with a wooden fork or spoon until they just start to form soft curds. Remove the pan from the heat and add the remaining butter and diced truffle. Stir until the egg mixture is still wet and soft. Remove from the heat.

5 Divide the slices of toast between the plates and spoon the scrambled eggs over the toast. Serve with a rocket or watercress salad, or on its own. Eat straight away and enjoy!

Conventional Cooking:
Cook on the hob and use a toaster or open flame to make the toast.

The best thing about having a fig tree in the garden is that it is both beautiful and productive. Figs are versatile as not only can you eat the fruit fresh from the tree, but you can also roast, poach, or preserve them in savoury and sweet recipes. You can also use the fig leaves to wrap up fish for grilling or baking, or you can use them to present food such as cheeses as part of a beautifully laid table. I eat the whole fig, skin and all, but this is a personal preference.

fig and cobnut salad

serves 6

150g cobnuts

5 large or 6 small ripe figs (not over-ripe)

olive oil

Frangelico liqueur

3 medium heads of chicory

100g seasonal salad leaves

6 generous slices of chewy sourdough bread

150g Caerphilly cheese, crumbled

FOR THE DRESSING:

2 tbsp groundnut oil

1 tbsp hazelnut oil

1 tbsp mild white wine vinegar

1 tsp honey

1 tsp Dijon mustard

salt and pepper

1 Roast the cobnuts on a baking tray on the first set of runners in the Roasting Oven for 2 minutes. Let them cool, then crack them in half.

2 Cut the figs into quarters, spread them on a baking tray and rub or brush a little olive oil and Frangelico on them. Roast them in the Roasting Oven for 5–8 minutes or until they are just starting to char around the edges.

3 Make the dressing while the figs are roasting by whisking all the ingredients together. Set aside.

4 Mix the green leaves in a bowl, spoon over 2 tablespoons of the dressing and toss well.

5 Toast the bread and place one slice on each plate. Divide the dressed leaves among the slices of toast and top each pile of leaves with some fig quarters, crumbled cheese and cobnuts. Spoon over a little more dressing and serve.

Conventional Cooking:
Roast the nuts and figs in an oven pre-heated to 200°C/400°F/gas 6.

Pâté is delicious and simple to make. To save time, I make pâtés by pan frying and whizzing in a processor rather than cooking in a bain-marie. Careful seasoning is vital to a good pâté as it is served cold. Chilled foods can stand a little more salt as the taste will dull when cool.

chicken liver pâté

serves 8–10

500g chicken livers, picked over and any green bits removed

milk, for soaking

1 rasher bacon, chopped or cubed

175g unsalted butter

1 red onion, peeled and finely chopped

1 garlic clove, peeled and crushed

1 tsp fresh thyme leaves

salt and pepper

2 tbsp Marsala

50–60g clarified butter, melted (see below)

1 Soak the chicken livers in some milk for about 30 minutes. Drain the chicken livers and discard the milk.

2 In a heavy-based frying pan on the Simmering Plate, fry the bacon until cooked but not too crispy. Remove from the pan and set aside.

3 Drain off the fat and melt about a tablespoon of the unsalted butter in the pan on the Simmering Plate. Put the rest of the butter into a bowl and leave to melt at the back of the Aga. Add the onions to the pan and cook on the floor of the Roasting Oven until soft.

4 Transfer the pan to the Simmering Plate and add the drained chicken livers, garlic and thyme leaves. Season with salt and pepper and cook for 5–7 minutes or until the chicken livers are well cooked all the way through.

5 Spoon the mix into a food processor and add the bacon. Deglaze the frying pan on the Simmering Plate with the Marsala, scraping up all the bits from the bottom of the pan. Add this to the food processor bowl along with the rest of the melted butter sitting at the back of the Aga. Blitz the pâté until it is smooth.

6 Check the seasoning again and, using a spatula, turn the pâté out into an earthenware dish. The dish must be big enough to have a 3cm gap at the top so that you can pour in the clarified butter. Leave the pâté to cool for about 30 minutes, then melt the clarified butter and pour over the top of the pâté. Add a few thyme leaves to garnish if you wish.

7 Cool until the butter has set, then cover with cling film and chill in the fridge. It is better to make the pâté a day in advance and let the flavours mingle. Serve with crusty bread, a wedge of lemon and redcurrant jelly.

Conventional Cooking:
Cook in a frying pan on the hob.

clarified butter

To make clarified butter, put the butter in a bowl or jug and leave at the back of the Aga. When the butter has melted, drain off all the clear yellow liquid leaving behind the white solids. You only want the clear yellow bit so discard the rest.

sausages with apples and smoked applewood cheese

serves 6

12 really good sausages

4 tbsp apple sauce (see below)

2 red apples, cored and thinly sliced into rings

125g smoked applewood cheese or Montgomery Cheddar cheese, grated

handful of breadcrumbs

1 Line a shallow baking tin with Bake-O-Glide and place the sausages on it. Do not prick them. Slide the tin on to the top set of runners in the Roasting Oven and cook for 8–10 minutes.

2 Remove the tin from the oven and slice the sausages open lengthways. Spoon the apple sauce over the split sausages and spread the apple rings on top. Scatter over the cheese and breadcrumbs.

3 Return the tin to the first or second set of runners in the Roasting Oven and continue to cook for another 8–10 minutes or until the cheese has melted and starts to brown on top. Serve with mashed potatoes.

Conventional Cooking:
Pre-heat the oven to 180°C/350°F/gas 4 and cook as above.

apple sauce

serves 6

1kg apples
sugar to taste
knob of butter

1 Peel and core the apples and cut into chunks. Put the apples into a saucepan with a splash of water (or use organic apple juice). Add about 2 tablespoons of sugar to start with, or less if you prefer a tarter sauce.

2 Heat the sauce on the Boiling Plate for few minutes, stirring all the time and being careful to prevent it from burning. Cover the pan with a tight fitting lid and transfer to the Simmering Oven for 30–60 minutes or until the apple has completely dissolved into a fluffy mass. Stir in the butter. Taste for sweetness and cool.

Conventional Cooking:
Cook on the hob.

sticky sausages with roasted garlic mash

serves 4–6

1 head of garlic

olive oil

6 large potatoes, peeled and cut into chunks

salt and pepper

250g butter

2 tbsp crème fraîche

2 packs of really good organic sausages

150ml organic honey

150ml organic blood orange marmalade

1 Place the whole head of garlic on a piece of foil large enough to wrap it in and pour over a little olive oil. Wrap it up tightly and roast it in the Roasting Oven for about 20–25 minutes or until it is soft. Remove it from the oven and let it cool until you are able to handle it. Squeeze out the flesh and mash it in a bowl, then set aside.

2 Meanwhile, fill a large saucepan with water, add salt and the potatoes and bring up to a boil on the Boiling Plate for 4 minutes. Drain away all the water, cover with a lid and transfer to the Simmering Oven for 20–25 minutes or until the potatoes are soft.

3 Using a potato ricer, mash the potatoes until smooth. Add the butter, garlic, salt and pepper to taste and the crème fraîche and beat well. Stir in a little olive oil until it is a dipping consistency rather than a stiff mash. Check the seasoning and either use straight away or set aside and reheat later when the sausages are ready.

4 Put the sausages into a roasting tin lined with Bake-O-Glide. Pour over the honey and marmalade and cook in the Roasting Oven for 20–25 minutes or until the sausages are crispy and bubbling. Serve with the garlic mash.

Conventional Cooking:

Cook the potatoes on the hob. Pre-heat the oven to 200°C/400°F/gas 6 and cook the sausages as above.

Note:

The mashed potatoes can be prepared ahead of time if you wish. If you don't have a potato ricer, do buy one as they are excellent and produce really smooth mash (or use a traditional potato masher).

shoulder of pork with chilli and sage

serves 6

2.5kg shoulder of pork, bone in
and trimmed of excess fat

1 large handful of fresh sage
leaves

1 red chilli

2 garlic cloves, peeled and
crushed

red pepper flakes

salt and pepper

splash of olive oil

250ml verjuice (see note), or
lemon juice and water

1 The day before, wipe the shoulder of pork dry and score the skin with a very sharp knife. Chop the sage leaves and the red chilli. In a bowl, mix the sage, chilli, garlic, a teaspoon or less (depending how hot or large the chilli is) of the pepper flakes, salt and pepper, and a splash of olive oil and really rub the mix into the top of the pork between the cuts on the shoulder. Cover and refrigerate overnight.

2 The next day, remove the pork from the fridge at least 30 minutes before cooking to allow it to come to room temperature. Put it into an earthenware dish with the marinade and roast on the third or fourth set of runners in the Roasting Oven for 1 hour. Pour the verjuice over the pork and move to the Simmering Oven for another 4–4½ hours or until tender and succulent.

3 Bubble up any pan juices and serve alongside. Carve and serve with roasted or mashed potato and smoked chilli jelly.

Conventional Cooking:
Pre-heat the oven to 180°C/350°F/gas 4 and cook for 3½–4½ hours.

Note:
Verjuice is more mellow than lemon juice and is made from grapes. You can buy it in good delis. Remember to allow enough time for the marinating.

bacon, chestnut and wild mushroom penne

serves 6

150g bacon cubes

knob of butter

375g mixed wild mushrooms

1 tsp thyme leaves

pinch of dried chilli flakes

500g penne pasta

Parmesan cheese

50g vacuum-packed chestnuts,
crumbled

salt and pepper

1 Fry the bacon cubes in a large heavy-bottomed saucepan on the Simmering Plate until they are crispy. Drain on kitchen towel and set aside.

2 Add a little butter to the bacon fat and fry the mushrooms along with the thyme and chilli flakes until soft.

3 Meanwhile, cook the penne on the Simmering or Boiling Plate in a large pan of rapidly boiling salted water until al dente. Drain but reserve some of the cooking water.

4 Add the pasta to the mushrooms along with some of the cooking liquid – not too much, just enough to loosen the mixture. Grate over lots of Parmesan, stir in some more butter and add the chestnuts. Check the seasoning and serve.

Conventional Cooking:
Cook on the hob.

Please eat more game – it is the only truly seasonal meat we have nowadays. On the whole it tends to be lean and therefore a healthy meat to eat. It is so tasty, and it's also cheap if you buy it directly from your local shoot.

roasted pheasant with quince cheese

serves 2

1 red onion, peeled
60g quince cheese (see page 149)
1 pheasant, not trussed
30g butter, softened
4 sprigs of fresh rosemary
1 tbsp flour
250ml good chicken stock
salt and pepper

1 Slice the onion thickly and lay on the bottom of a roasting tin. Put half the quince cheese into the pheasant cavity and season with salt and pepper. Smear the butter over the bird and season. Lay the pheasant over the onions and tuck two of the rosemary sprigs into the tin.

2 Roast on the third set of runners in the Roasting Oven for 20–25 minutes or until the juices run clear when the thigh is poked with a skewer.

3 Remove the pheasant from the oven. Lift out the bird and carefully tip so that any quince cheese left in the cavity runs into the pan juices. Move the pheasant to a warmed plate, cover with foil and let it rest while you make the gravy.

4 Skim off the excess fat from the tin, leaving about a tablespoon behind and whisk in the flour until it is absorbed. If you prefer thinner gravy, add less flour. Gradually add the stock and bring it to the boil on the Boiling Plate, then let it all simmer for 2–3 minutes. Chop the remaining rosemary leaves very finely. Strain the gravy into a warmed jug and add the rosemary.

5 Serve the pheasant with the gravy. Keep the vegetables light, such as French beans and a few small roasted potatoes.

Conventional Cooking
Pre-heat the oven to 220°C/425°F/gas 7 and cook as above.

Pomegranates appear from September through to December. The fruit doesn't ripen after it's picked and there are no external indications of ripeness so try to buy organic fruit, heavy for its size as it should have more seeds and less bitter membrane.

pomegranate and pheasant salad

serves 6

2 pheasants
butter
3 pomegranates
85g cobnuts or walnut pieces
1 head of frisee lettuce
1 bunch of watercress
2–3 heads of chicory

FOR THE DRESSING:
1 tbsp red wine vinegar
1 tbsp walnut oil
2 tbsp sunflower oil
1 tsp organic honey
salt and pepper

1 To roast the pheasants, put them into a roasting tin and smear with butter. Roast them for 40–50 minutes in the Roasting Oven or until cooked, then leave to cool.

2 Meanwhile, make the dressing. Mix all the ingredients together in a screw-top jar and shake vigorously or whisk together in a bowl. Set aside.

3 Shred the meat from the pheasant and if the skin is crispy, shred that too. Put the meat into a large bowl.

4 Slice the pomegranates in half. Hold cut side down over the pheasant bowl, tap the top with a wooden spoon and the seeds should fall out. Add the nuts to the bowl and spoon over half the dressing. Mix everything well and check the seasoning.

5 In another large bowl mix the greens together. At this point you can either pile the pheasant on top of the greens in the bowl, or arrange it on one large platter, or assemble each individual plate with a pile of greens and the pheasant and pomegranates on top and drizzle over a little more dressing. Serve any extra dressing on the side. Serve with crusty peasant bread

Conventional Cooking:
Pre-heat the oven to 200°C/400°F/gas 6 and roast the pheasants as above.

pan-fried pigeon breasts with maltaise sauce

serves 6

2–3 tbsp flour

salt and pepper

12 pigeon breasts (2 per person)

clarified butter (see page 118)

1 orange, segmented

watercress to garnish

FOR THE MALTAISE SAUCE:

2 large organic egg yolks

juice of ½ a lemon

1 tbsp water

salt and white pepper

250g unsalted butter, cut into cubes

juice and zest of 1 organic orange

1 To make the sauce, place the egg yolks, lemon juice, water, salt and pepper in a bowl over a pan of simmering water (do not let the bowl come into contact with the water) and whisk until the mix leaves a ribbon trail. Do this on the Simmering Plate. Whisking constantly, drop in the cubes of butter one at a time – don't drop in the next cube until the previous one has been absorbed. This will take some time.

2 Meanwhile, in another small pan, reduce the juice of the orange together with the zest by half. When all the butter is used and you have a thick velvety sauce, add the reduced orange juice and zest. Taste for seasoning. Keep the sauce warm at the side of the Aga.

3 Season the flour with salt and pepper and put it on to a flattish plate. Dust the pigeon breasts in it and shake off the excess.

4 Heat a heavy frying pan in the Roasting Oven until it is searingly hot. Remove it from the oven and continue on the Simmering or Boiling Plate. Melt about a tablespoon of clarified butter in it and fry the pigeon breasts in batches for 2 minutes each side or longer, to your liking.

5 Drain the meat on kitchen paper and rest for 5 minutes in a warm place.

6 Slice the breasts and arrange on a warm plate. Spoon over some of the sauce and garnish with watercress and an orange segment.

Conventional Cooking:

Cook on the hob.

roast partridge with apples and pears

serves 6

12 shallots, peeled
6 partridges, oven ready
salt and pepper
1 apple, cut into 6 pieces
clarified butter (see page 118)
100ml Calvados
600ml home-made game stock
80g dried organic pear pieces

1 Cut the shallots in half and place cut side down in a roasting tin.

2 Season the inside of the birds with salt and put an apple piece inside each one. Place the partridges on top of the shallots. Brush over a little clarified butter and season the birds with salt and pepper. Cook on the fourth set of runners in the Roasting Oven for 15–20 minutes.

3 When they are cooked, remove the apple pieces from the cavity of the birds and put into the tin. Transfer the partridges to a warmed platter, cover with foil and let the birds rest for 15 minutes (this is imperative).

4 Meanwhile, finish the sauce. Put the roasting tin on the Boiling Plate (or Simmering Plate if the heat it too vigorous). Deglaze with the Calvados and add the stock. Bring to a boil and reduce the sauce for about 3–4 minutes. Check the sauce for seasoning.

5 When you are ready to serve, strain the sauce through a sieve and add the pears to the sauce for about 1 minute – just to heat through. Place each partridge on a warmed plate and spoon over the sauce.

Conventional Cooking:
Pre-heat the oven to 180°C/350°F/gas 4 and cook the partridges as above. Finish the sauce on the hob.

shredded chicken with polenta and wild mushrooms

serves 6

6 chicken legs
olive oil
zest and juice of one lemon
salt and pepper
lemon thyme
clarified butter (see page 118)
100g mixed wild mushrooms
½ garlic clove, peeled and crushed
flat leaf parsley
6 long slices of polenta
75g rocket
75g beet tops

1 Put the chicken legs into a sealable plastic bag, add some olive oil, the lemon zest, salt and pepper and a few sprigs of lemon thyme, then marinate in the fridge overnight.

2 Drain the chicken legs from the marinade and put them in a roasting tin. Season with salt and pepper. Place the tin on the second or third runners in the Roasting Oven and roast for 25–35 minutes or until the meat is falling off the bones.

3 Remove the chicken from the tin and set aside to cool. When cool enough to handle, shred the meat from the bone using your hands. Put the meat into a bowl and set aside.

4 Make the dressing by whisking 1 tablespoon lemon juice, 3 tablespoons olive oil, salt and pepper together. Spoon some of the dressing into the shredded meat.

5 Heat some olive oil in a large frying pan with some clarified butter on the Simmering Plate. Add the wild mushrooms and gently fry until they are soft. Add the crushed garlic, parsley and a sprig of lemon thyme and cook for a few more minutes. Do not let the garlic burn. Remove from the Simmering Plate and set at the back or side of the Aga to keep warm.

6 Heat a large griddle pan on the Roasting Oven floor until it is smoking and then transfer it to the Boiling Plate. Place the polenta slices in the pan and char on both sides.

7 Toss the rocket and beet tops together. Arrange the polenta slices on a large platter and top each one with some of the leaves. Mix the shredded chicken meat with the mushrooms and divide the mix over the leaves. Drizzle over the remaining dressing and serve.

Conventional Cooking:
Pre-heat the oven to 200°C/400°F/gas 6 and roast the chicken legs for 35–40 minutes or until the meat is falling off the bone. Cook the mushrooms and polenta slices in a griddle pan on the hob.

Note:
You can make your polenta ahead of time, leave to dry and slice, or buy readymade polenta and slice it yourself.

roast duck with pumpkin sage mash

serves 4

2 large ducks, each approximately 2.5kg (you will need half a duck per person)

brandy

2 oranges

2kg pumpkin, deseeded and cut into long thick slices

olive oil

8 finely chopped fresh sage leaves

salt and pepper

1kg Desiree potatoes, peeled and chopped into small pieces

1 whole clove, crushed very finely with a pestle and mortar

freshly grated nutmeg

200g mascarpone cheese

unsalted butter

bottled damsons

1 Put one of the ducks into a colander and pour over a kettle of boiling water to help the fat to loosen. Drain and dry the duck thoroughly with kitchen paper inside and out. Repeat with the second duck. Brush the ducks with a little brandy (alcohol helps to dry out the skin, giving you a crispier finish).

2 Hang the ducks up by the wings with a plate underneath in a place with a cool breeze (the air helps to keep the duck really dry). If you don't have anywhere suitable, put them uncovered into the fridge. This can all be done a day in advance, but they must be left hanging for a minimum of 6 hours.

3 To cook the ducks, slice one of the oranges into wedges and stuff the wedges into the cavity of the ducks. Put the ducks on a grill rack in a roasting tin and hang it on the second or third set of runners in the Roasting Oven. Cook for 1–2 hours, depending how big the ducks are. I like the meat almost falling away from the bones and really crispy skin, but if you want your duck rarer, only cook it for about an hour. You can also cook the duck in the Roasting Oven for 40–45 minutes, then move it to the Simmering Oven for 2–3 hours so that it has a longer, slower cooking time. This also gives a wonderfully moist inside with an outer crispness. When the ducks have finished cooking, remove from the oven and allow to rest for 5–10 minutes

4 To make the mash, place the slices of pumpkin on a shallow roasting tray. Drizzle over olive oil, sprinkle over the sage and season. Roast on the second set of runners in the Roasting Oven for 20 minutes or until the flesh is very soft.

5 Meanwhile, put the potatoes into a pan of boiling water on the Boiling Plate and cook for 5 minutes. Drain off all the water, cover with a lid, move them to the Simmering Oven and cook for 15–20 minutes or until very tender.

6 Scrape the flesh from the pumpkin skin, place in a bowl and mash with a fork. Push the cooked potatoes through a potato ricer into the bowl with the pumpkin. Grate over the zest of the remaining orange, and add the crushed garlic and a little grated nutmeg. Add the mascarpone cheese and mix well. Taste for seasoning – you will probably need to add salt. If it is too stiff, add a little olive oil or butter. (These quantities will make extra mash so you will have some left over. The mash can be made ahead of time. To reheat, put a knob of butter into a pan on the Simmering Plate, fold in the mash and heat.)

7 Serve each person with half a duck and some pumpkin mash, with some bottled damsons.

Conventional Cooking:
Pre-heat the oven to 200°C/400°F/gas 6 and roast the ducks for 1½–2 hours until crispy. Boil the potatoes on the hob. Roast the pumpkin at 200°C/400°F/gas 6 for 25–30 minutes or until the flesh is very soft.

I think most fish should be cooked very quickly and simply. I am all for just a splash of wine or lemon juice and fresh herbs. However, this porcini dust is fab as you can make it and dust it over lots of different fish, and how great to combine wild mushrooms with an autumn fish such as skate. Simply made for each other!

skate wings with porcini powder

serves 4

50g dried porcini mushrooms

60g clarified butter (see page 118)

4 skate wings (if you don't want to deal with the bones, ask your fishmonger for skate wing fillets)

salt

truffle oil, for drizzling

1 To make the porcini dust, use a coffee grinder or a spice grinder. Whiz up the dried porcini and sieve to get a very fine powder. (To clean out coffee grinders after grinding spices, whiz up a piece of bread to clean the blades.)

2 Heat the butter in a frying pan on the Simmering Plate until it is frothing. Dust the skate wings lightly with the porcini powder and season with salt.

3 Fry the skate wings on the Simmering Plate for 2 minutes per side – you may have to do this in batches (if using fillets, fry for only 1 minute per side). Plate up and drizzle with the truffle oil. Serve with mashed potatoes.

Conventional Cooking:
Cook on the hob.

pancetta-wrapped prawns

serves 6

18 king prawns, de-veined and shelled

18 slices pancetta

olive oil

butter

brandy

1 Soak 18 cocktail sticks in water before using them.

2 Wrap each king prawn in a slice of pancetta and secure in place with a cocktail stick.

3 Heat some olive oil and a little butter in a frying pan on the Boiling Plate. When it is sizzling, sauté the prawns in batches, then transfer to a plate and keep warm until they are all cooked. If the Boiling Plate is too fierce, move the pan to the Simmering Plate.

4 Deglaze the pan with a slug of brandy and pour over the prawns. Serve with rice.

Conventional Cooking:
Cook on the hob.

pancetta-wrapped prawns

autumn pizza

Either use my suggestions for the pizza topping or use whatever vegetables are in season.

makes 2 pizzas

FOR THE PIZZA DOUGH:

40g fresh yeast

125ml milk, at room temperature

175ml hand-hot water

300g '00' flour

40g strong plain flour

3g salt

olive oil, for greasing the bowl

FOR THE TOPPING:

ricotta cheese

marinated artichokes, drained and sliced

sliced mushrooms

thyme

chilli flakes

Manchego cheese, sliced

olive oil

1 Prove the yeast with the milk and water by crumbling the yeast into the liquid and leaving for 10 minutes.

2 Mix the yeast with the sifted flours and salt and knead for 10 minutes – the dough should be sticky.

3 Knead the dough for a further 10 minutes, adding more flour if necessary. Whatever happens do not end up with a stable dough – it should be threatening to stick to the bowl. Tip the dough into an oiled bowl and leave to rise in a warm place, close to the Aga, for about 1 hour or until doubled in size.

4 Shape the dough into a pizza shape by pulling and stretching it; do not roll. Let it rise for about 10 minutes.

5 Spread over the ricotta cheese, then scatter over the sliced artichokes, sliced mushrooms, thyme, chilli flakes and Manchego cheese. Bake on the floor of the Roasting Oven for 12–15 minutes.

Conventional Cooking:

Pre-heat the oven to its highest setting and use a baking stone (follow the manufacturer's instructions).

Risottos are wonderful. I think they were originally peasant food using local seasonal ingredients, so almost anything goes! Making a risotto in the traditional way is not suited to an Aga unless you are not cooking anything else for a while (the 20 minutes' cooking time would kill off a lot of stored heat) but my Aga method is easy and even a hardened purist (who shall remain nameless!) had to admit that my risotto is the business. Butter and Parmesan are what make a really delicious risotto, so use the best of both and be generous.

pumpkin risotto

serves 6–8

olive oil

1 onion, peeled and finely chopped

salt and pepper

1 garlic clove, peeled and finely chopped

280g arborio risotto rice

1 glass white wine

850ml stock, heated

100g grated Parmesan cheese

250g pumpkin purée (tinned organic purée is fine or make it yourself)

generous knob of butter

1 tsp fresh thyme leaves

1 Pour a tablespoon of olive oil into a heavy-bottomed frying pan and place it on the floor of the Roasting Oven to heat up. When it is hot, add the onion and put back on the Roasting Oven floor to soften.

2 When the onion is ready, place the pan on the Simmering Plate. Season with salt and pepper, add the garlic and risotto rice and, stirring the entire time, coat the rice in the onion and oil mixture until the rice is translucent. Pour in the wine and stir until it is almost all evaporated, then add all the stock, stir and bring to the boil. Place the uncovered pan on the fourth set of runners in the Roasting Oven for 20–25 minutes (I like to check it after 10 minutes and stir).

3 When the liquid has nearly all been absorbed and the rice is tender but still has a bit of a bite, take the pan out of the oven and stir in the Parmesan, pumpkin purée, knob of butter and thyme.

4 Put the pan on the Simmering Plate and stir for about 5 minutes to melt the cheese and heat up the purée. Add more butter to serve. If it is too stiff, add more stock. Check the seasoning and serve with a green salad.

Conventional Cooking:

Make the risotto in the conventional way on the hob with a bubbling pot of stock and ladle it into the rice little by little and stir constantly. Do not add the next ladle of stock until the last one is absorbed – it will take you about 20 minutes.

Wild mushrooms are a great treat in the autumn and if you live near an area where you can collect them, find out the picking rules from your local forest rangers. I always advise people to go gathering with an expert as results can be fatal from just one wrong mushroom. Always buy or gather only what you need for one meal – mushrooms should be eaten as fresh as possible as they are living fungi and decompose quickly. Do not put mushrooms in plastic; keep them in an open basket or a brown paper bag as the air should circulate around them. Do not choose mushrooms with black spots or bruises. Before cooking them, use a soft natural bristle brush to brush any dirt from the surface or gills. Wipe them with a damp cloth – do not submerge them in water as they can easily become waterlogged.

wild mushroom risotto with crispy sage leaves

serves 6

sunflower oil

6 large sage leaves

olive oil

1 onion, peeled and finely chopped

450g wild mushrooms, such as porcini, chanterelle, oyster or trompette, sliced

salt and pepper

1 garlic clove, peeled and finely chopped

1 sprig thyme, leaves stripped

500g arborio risotto rice

1 glass white wine

1 litre chicken stock, warmed

200g Parmesan cheese, grated

generous knob of butter

1 tbsp chopped fresh herbs – choose your favourites

1 Heat some sunflower oil in a shallow frying pan on the floor of the Roasting Oven until the oil starts to smoke. Drop in the sage leaves, fry until crispy, then drain on kitchen paper and set aside.

2 Put 1 tablespoon of olive oil into a heavy-bottomed frying pan and place it on the floor of the Roasting Oven to heat up. When it is hot, add the onion and mushrooms and put it back on the Roasting Oven floor to soften them.

3 When the onion and mushrooms are ready, place the pan on the Simmering Plate and add salt and pepper, the garlic, thyme leaves and risotto rice. Stirring all the time, coat the rice in the onion and oil mixture until the rice is translucent. Pour in the wine and stir until it has almost all evaporated, then add all the stock and stir. Bring to the boil, then place the pan on the fourth set of runners in the Roasting Oven for 20–25 minutes. When the liquid has nearly all been absorbed and the rice is tender but still has a bit of a bite, take the pan out of the oven and stir in the Parmesan, a knob of butter and the fresh herbs.

4 Check the seasoning and serve each portion of risotto with a fried sage leaf on top.

Conventional Cooking:
Fry the sage leaves and the onion and mushrooms on the hob. Cook the risotto on the hob.

Note:
If you use dried mushrooms in this recipe, soak them in boiling water for about 10 minutes or until soft, then strain, reserving the liquid to use with or instead of the stock.

ACCOMPANIMENTS

Nothing delights me more than a big pumpkin – I think they are a very cheery vegetable and so versatile. You can mash them, roast or chunk them, and use them for savoury or sweet dishes. Try to grow them yourself – you do need a bit of space but they are easy to grow.

roasted pumpkin

serves 6

1 pumpkin, deseeded and sliced into long quarters

mild olive oil

dried red chillies flakes – as much as you like, I use just a pinch

1 fat garlic clove, peeled and thinly sliced

salt and pepper

150–175g chorizo sausages (about 4), sliced

1 Place the pumpkin slices on a shallow roasting tray, drizzle over olive oil and sprinkle chilli flakes, garlic slices, salt and pepper. Roast on the second set of runners in the Roasting Oven for 20 minutes or until the flesh is soft.

2 Put the chorizo sausages in a small frying pan with 1 tablespoon olive oil and fry either on the Roasting Oven floor or on the Boiling or Simmering Plate. Drain the chorizo and set aside. When the pumpkin is coated, add the chorizo to the roasting tin and stir through the pumpkin slices.

Conventional cooking:
Pre-heat the oven to 220°C/425°F/gas 7 and roast the pumpkin for 25–30 minutes or until the flesh is very soft. Fry the chorizo on the hob.

portobello mushrooms with parsley and garlic

serves 6

6 Portobello mushrooms, stalks removed

olive oil

knob of butter

2 shallots, peeled and finely chopped

250g oyster mushrooms, sliced in half

100g button mushrooms, chopped

150g mixed wild mushrooms (halve or quarter if very large or leave whole if small)

2 garlic cloves, peeled and crushed

1 tbsp lemon thyme leaves

1 tbsp chopped fresh flat leaf parsley

juice of ½ a lemon, plus the zest

1 heaped tbsp crème fraîche

salt and pepper

1 Lay the Portobello mushrooms on a large shallow baking tray, drizzle over some olive oil and season with salt and pepper. Slide the tray on to the second set of runners in the Roasting Oven and cook for about 10 minutes or until they are just soft.

2 While they are cooking, heat up about 1 tablespoon of olive oil and the knob of butter in a frying pan on the Simmering Plate. Cook the shallots until soft then add the remaining mushrooms, garlic, lemon thyme, parsley, salt and pepper and juice and zest of the lemon. Don't let the garlic burn.

3 After 5–8 minutes, when the mushrooms are tender, stir in the crème fraîche and simmer for 2 minutes to let the sauce thicken.

4 Take the Portobello mushrooms out of the oven and put one on each plate. Spoon some of the wild mushroom mix on to each mushroom and sprinkle over a little more chopped parsley. Serve with crusty bread.

Conventional Cooking:
Pre-heat the oven to 200°C/400°F/gas 6 and continue as above for the mushrooms. Cook the filling on the hob.

roasted pumpkin

DESSERTS AND BAKING

Damsons are part of the plum family and a superb fruit to preserve. They are one of my husband's favourite puddings – bottled damsons in port, served cold with lashings of double cream. Damson cheese (see page 149), made in the same way as quince cheese, is delicious with lamb or game. You don't come across bullace very much but they are related to the plum/sloe/damson family. Use them in the same way as damsons.

damsons in distress

serves 4

500g ripe organic damsons
220g golden caster sugar
125ml port, plus more for topping up
100ml water

1 Wash and dry the damsons and discard any bruised or mouldy ones.
2 Put the sugar, port and water into a saucepan and bring to the boil on the Boiling Plate for 2–3 minutes. Add the fruit to the syrup, return to the boil and cook for 5–7 minutes.
3 Pack the fruit into sterilised wide-mouthed jars using a slotted spoon and pour in the hot stock syrup so that the jar is half-full. Top up with more port to fill the jars within 3cm of the top. Seal and store in a dark place for a minimum of 2 months – don't be tempted to eat them earlier!

Conventional Cooking:
Cook on the hob.

We have a huge quince tree in our garden and it is a delight to make quince cheese (see page 149), or use quinces with apples for added colour and flavour.

poached quinces in pudding wine

serves 6

1 bottle of sweet pudding wine – something with orange overtones would be perfect
150ml water
120g golden caster sugar
6 quinces, peeled with stems intact

1 Put the wine, water and sugar in a large saucepan. Bring up to the boil on the Boiling Plate and stir until the sugar dissolves. Add the quinces. Cover with a lid and simmer for 45–60 minutes in the Simmering Oven or until tender.
2 Remove the pan from the oven and cool the quinces in the liquid for about 20 minutes, turning them from time to time.
3 Using a slotted spoon, transfer the quinces to a dish. Sieve the poaching liquor into a clean saucepan and bring back to the boil on the Boiling Plate, then simmer on the Simmering Plate to reduce until syrupy. Pour the syrup over the quinces and set aside to cool. Serve with the syrup and thick cream.

Conventional Cooking:
Poach the quinces on the hob over a medium heat.

baked apples with cinnamon crumble topping

serves 6

6 Bramley apples
1 punnet of blackberries
1 tbsp golden caster sugar

FOR THE CRUMBLE TOPPING:
180g plain flour
90g cold unsalted butter
½ tsp ground cinnamon
90g golden granulated sugar
60g roasted chopped almonds
demerara sugar, for topping

1 To make the crumble topping, sift the flour into a bowl and rub in the butter until it resembles coarse breadcrumbs. Stir in the cinnamon, sugar and half the almonds.

2 Core the apples, scooping out a good chunk of the centres, but leaving the bottom third intact.

3 Mix the blackberries and sugar together in a bowl. Divide the blackberries between the apples, spooning them into the centres to come halfway up the apples, then spoon over the crumble mix. Sprinkle the crumble with the rest of the almonds and some demerara sugar.

4 Put the apples on a shallow baking tray and slide on to the fourth set of runners in the Roasting Oven for 35–45 minutes or until they are done – this will depend on the size of the apples. Check the apples after 25–30 minutes – if they are browning too much, slide in the Cold Plain Shelf. If you have a Baking Oven, you can bake them for 40–50 minutes as above.

Conventional Cooking:
Pre-heat the oven to 200°C/400°F/gas 6 and continue as above.

Note:
Serve these with lashings of double cream or custard or vanilla ice cream, or all three!

pear and orange crunch

serves 4

4 pears, peeled, cored and sliced into wedges
6 tbsp unsalted butter
juice of 1 orange
zest of ½ orange (peel with a very sharp knife and cut into thin strips)
50g sultanas, steeped in boiling water for 10 minutes
4 tbsp flour
8 tbsp Muscovado sugar

1 Arrange the pears in an ovenproof dish. Dot with ½ tablespoon of butter and pour over the orange juice, zest and sultanas.

2 Rub the flour into 1 tablespoon of butter and then mix in the sugar. The topping is literally just a 'crunch'. Scatter it over the pears – it should be light and crispy, not heavy and thick.

3 Put the dish on to the third set of runners in the Roasting Oven and bake for 20–25 minutes or until the pears are just soft and the topping is crunchy. If you wish, brown the top with a blow-torch.

Conventional Cooking:
Pre-heat the oven to 180°C/°350 F/gas 4 and cook for 30–35 minutes. Brown with a blow-torch or under a hot grill.

caramel apples

makes 4 or 6

240g granulated sugar
120ml corn syrup
120ml condensed milk
60ml double cream
118ml milk
30g unsalted butter
1 tsp vanilla extract
4 large crisp apples or 6 small ones
235g chopped pecan nuts

1 Combine the sugar, corn syrup, condensed milk, cream, milk and butter in a medium saucepan. Place on the Simmering Plate and stir constantly until the mixture reaches the hard ball stage on a sugar thermometer
2 Stir in the vanilla extract and then put the pan over a very gentle heat (the Aga warming plate is perfect for this).
3 Insert the wooden sticks into the stem ends of the apples. Dip the apples into the caramel sauce. Allow the excess to drip off over the pan. Roll the apples in the chopped nuts and let them cool on a piece of Bake-O-Glide.

Conventional Cooking:
Make the caramel on the hob.

Note:
Use forks, wooden ice cream sticks or garden twigs to 'serve' the apples.

apple custard

serves 4

60g caster sugar
250ml water
1 cinnamon stick
2 apples, peeled, cored and cut into thick slices

FOR THE BAKED CUSTARD:
2 organic eggs, plus 4 organic egg yolks
300ml milk
200ml cream
1 scraped vanilla pod or 1 tsp vanilla extract
115g golden caster sugar
frshly grated nutmeg

1 Put the sugar, water and cinnamon stick into a saucepan and heat on the Simmering Plate until the sugar has dissolved. Add the apple slices and continue to simmer for 4–5 minutes. Remove the apples with a slotted spoon and place in an ovenproof dish.
2 Make the custard. In a bowl, whisk together the eggs, yolks and sugar, then set aside. Pour the milk and cream into a pan. Scrape the vanilla pod seeds into the milk and add the sugar. Gently bring to a simmer on the Simmering Plate. Take the milk off the heat and add to the egg yolk mix, little by little, whisking constantly. Using a sieve, pour the custard over the apples. Grate the nutmeg on top.
3 Put the dish on to a baking tray and slide on to the third or fourth runners in the Simmering Oven. Cook for 1–2 hours or until it is set. Serve with more thick cream if desired and more caster sugar.

Conventional Cooking:
Cook the custard and apple on the hob. Bake the custard in a water bath: pre-heat the oven to 160°C/325°F/gas 3, place the dish into a roasting tin, adding hot water to come halfway up the dish. Bake for 1 hour or until set.

Note:
This recipe also works well with pears.

caramel apples

roasted plums with taleggio cheese

serves 8

50g salted butter

8 ripe plums, stoned and cut in half

30g soft brown sugar

pepper

450g Taleggio cheese, at room temperature

1 Melt the butter in a dish at the back of the Aga.

2 Line a shallow baking tray with Bake-O-Glide. Place the plums cut side up on the baking tray and brush each one with the melted butter. Grind over some black pepper and sprinkle over the sugar.

3 Slide the tray on to the third set of runners in the Roasting Oven. Roast for 10 minutes, then move to the Simmering Oven and continue to cook for a further 40–60 minutes or until the plums start to caramelise at the edges and shrink to about half their original size.

4 When caramelised, arrange the plums on a plate and top each half with a slice of Taleggio.

Conventional Cooking:
Pre-heat the oven to 160°C/325°F/gas 3 and continue as above.

autumn berry cobbler

serves 4

500g autumn berries

100g sugar

3 tbsp flour

FOR THE COBBLER TOPPING:

145g self-raising flour

pinch of salt

2 tsp baking powder

90g cold unsalted butter cubes

20g golden caster sugar

120ml double cream, plus a little extra for brushing

1 First, make the cobbler topping. Put the flour, salt, baking powder, butter and sugar into a food processor. Pulse until the texture is similar to bread-crumbs. Add the cream and pulse again until it just starts to come together.

2 Turn the dough out on to a floured surface and roll to a thickness of 2cm. Use a cookie cutter to cut into rounds or a knife for squares. Re-roll the scraps and cut into the desired shapes. You need to have 8 biscuits.

3 Put the berries into a deep ovenproof dish and fold in the sugar and flour. Top the berries with the biscuits and brush the biscuits with some cream.

4 Place the dish on a shallow baking tray and slid the tray on to the fourth set of runners in the Roasting Oven (if you have a Baking Oven, do use it). Slide in the Cold Plain Shelf after 10–12 minutes. Continue to bake the cobbler for a further 20–25 minutes or until the biscuits are baked through and golden.

Conventional Cooking:
Pre-heat the oven to 180°C/350°F/gas 4 and bake as above.

Note:
Use whatever autumn berries you have to hand for this dessert. Serve with cold double cream and caster sugar.

roasted plums with taleggio cheese

This is my basic crumble topping mix to which I add or substitute many different things. You can be as adventurous as you like depending on the season and the combinations of fruit or vegetables available.

I make the sweet crumble topping with equal quantities of flour, butter and sugar. You can make it in 120g (small, 2–4 servings), 180g (medium, 4–6 servings) or 240g (large, 6–8 servings) proportions.

crumble toppings

serves 4–6

FOR THE BASIC SWEET CRUMBLE TOPPING:

180g plain flour

180g very cold unsalted butter

180g golden granulated sugar

brown sugar for the final topping

½ tsp spice, depending on the fruit (optional)

FOR THE BASIC SAVOURY CRUMBLE TOPPING:

180g plain flour

150g very cold butter

salt and pepper

100g cheese – Parmesan, Cheddar, or your choice, plus more for the final topping

1 tbsp chopped fresh herbs, depending on the filling

1 Butter an ovenproof dish. Put the fruit (or savoury filling) into a dish, add a little sugar if the fruit needs it.

2 In a roomy bowl, sift in the flour and rub in the butter. When the mix resembles coarse breadcrumbs, mix in the sugar and spice (or cheese, seasoning and herbs for the savoury version) – you can do this in a food processor but don't overdo it. Spoon the crumble topping over the filling and sprinkle over some more brown sugar for a sweet filling (or cheese for a savoury filling).

3 Put the dish into an Aga roasting tin, place on the fourth set of runners in the Roasting Oven and cook for 20–25 minutes, then transfer to the Simmering Oven and cook for a further 20–25 minutes or until the filling is tender and the topping is cooked. (For crumbles using soft fruits, cut the cooking time down to 20–25 minutes in Roasting Oven only.) For 4-oven Aga owners, use the third set of runners in the Baking Oven and cook for 35–45 minutes.

Conventional Cooking:

Pre-heat the oven to 180°C/350°F/gas 4 and bake the crumble for 30–40 minutes.

Crumble additions:

- Crushed biscuits: cut down the amount of flour and replace with the biscuits.
- Dried breadcrumbs such as brioche, panettone, croissant, malt loaf: substitute about half the flour for breadcrumbs.
- Cocoa powder: substitute about 1 heaped tablespoon of flour for really good organic cocoa powder.
- Using different sugar textures will give different results.
- Add different spices to the mixture.
- Shaved chocolate is delicious in the mix and sprinkled over the crumble as it comes out of the oven.
- Add herbs to savoury crumble toppings.
- Nuts: ground nuts give a gritty texture and nibbed or chopped give a crunchy texture.
- Pine nuts are delicious.
- Desiccated coconut is also wonderful.
- Cereals such as oatmeal, muesli, cornflakes or anything else you fancy. Use these for the final topping.
- For savoury crumbles use olive oil or flavoured oils.
- For savoury Indian-style crumble toppings, use breadcrumbs made from naan bread and use curry powder instead of spice.

Favourite fruit fillings:

- Rhubarb and stem ginger.
- Blackberries and figs.
- Blackberries and apples.
- Bananas and mango with a desiccated coconut topping.
- Pear and prune.
- Apricots, almonds and lavender liqueur.

Favourite savoury fillings:

- Tomato and courgette.
- Spinach with pine nuts, raisins and feta cheese crumble topping.
- Roasted pumpkin with cubed smoked bacon and Parmesan crumble topping.
- Marinated artichokes with focaccia breadcrumb and Gorgonzola cheese crumble topping.

I like English apples and have a few apple trees in our orchard – I have no idea of their variety, only that some are cookers and some are eaters! I love Granny Smith apples and nothing beats a trip out to an apple grower to taste the delights of old-fashioned varieties that are now so scarce. One thing to keep in mind when buying apples is that the later varieties are generally the best keepers and storing apples in a cold dark place without them touching is the best way to keep them. Use old-fashioned apple storage racks. Apples are generally described as dessert, cooking or cider, and personal taste will dictate what varieties you use. I just hate the woolly kind and avoid them like the plague!

apple cake

serves 8

230ml sunflower oil
30ml hazelnut oil
400g caster sugar
3 large eggs
1 tsp vanilla extract
470g plain flour
pinch of salt
1 tsp baking soda
2 tsp baking powder
1 tsp cinnamon
4 large cooking apples, peeled, cored and chopped into small cubes

1 Grease a deep 20.5cm cake tin (or 2 small loaf tins).

2 Mix the oils and sugar together in a food processor. Add the eggs one at a time, still mixing, and then add vanilla extract.

3 Sift all the dry ingredients together and fold into the eggy mix. Gently fold in the apples.

4 Pour the mixture into the prepared tin and bake for 15 minutes in the Roasting Oven, then move to the Simmering Oven and continue to bake for 1½–2 hours or until a skewer comes out clean.

For 2-oven Aga owners with a Cake Baker, bake for about 1 hour 25 minutes or until a skewer comes out clean.

For 4-oven Aga owners, bake in the Baking Oven for about 1 hour or until a skewer comes out clean.

5 Cool on a wire rack, then serve with thick double cream.

Conventional Cooking:
Pre-heat the oven to 180°C/350°F/gas 4 and bake for 1 hour.

Note:
Always save the paper that your butter comes wrapped in as it comes in very useful when baking. If things start to brown too quickly in the oven, simply place a butter wrapper on top. Store the wrappers in the fridge in a plastic bag until required.

PRESERVES

Everyone loves a freebie and blackberries are great because they are full of flavour, easy to pick and free! I wouldn't ever dream of buying blackberries as they are one of the last bastions of truly seasonally fruit. One of the best pie fillings is still blackberry and apple and the same goes for crumble.

oven-made raspberry and blackberry jam

makes about 4 jars

250g blackberries
250g autumn raspberries
440g golden caster sugar
1 tsp lemon juice

1 Put the berries into an ovenproof dish. Put the sugar into a separate ovenproof dish. Put a grid rack on the floor of the Roasting Oven and place both dishes on the grid rack for 20–30 minutes. The berries should still hold their shape – check after 20 minutes. The fruit and sugar should be very hot.
2 Very carefully combine the hot sugar and hot berries and lemon juice, and stir together. The berries will melt with the sugar, creating instant jam. Ladle into sterilised jam jars (see page 14) and seal.

Conventional Cooking:
Pre-heat the oven to 200°C/400°F/gas 6 and cook as above.

apple butter

makes about 6 jars

2.5kg sharp/tart apples,
200ml water
200ml unsweetened organic apple juice
soft brown sugar
1 tsp ground cinnamon
½ tsp ground cloves
pinch of ground allspice
zest and juice of 2 lemons

1 Peel, core and chop the apples, reserving the peel and cores. Put the peel and cores into a piece of muslin, wrap up and tie with butcher's string.
2 Put the apples, muslin bag of cores and peel, water and apple juice into a large stainless steel pot and bring to the boil on the Boiling Plate. Cook until soft.
3 Discard the muslin bag. Pass the apples through a sieve to make a smooth purée. Add 100g brown sugar to every 200g purée. Taste and adjust sugar to your liking. Put the purée back in the pot. Stir in spices, zest and lemon juice.
4 Place the pan on the Simmering Plate and gently reach a rapid simmer. Stir well and move to the Simmering Oven for 2–4 hours, stirring every hour until dark and thick. Pour into sterilised jars and seal. Will keep for 6 months.

Conventional Cooking:
Cook on the hob.

Note:
No, it's not a mistake – there is no butter in this recipe! Serve this with toast or crumpets, or spread on bread or pancakes for breakfast or at teatime.

damson cheese

makes about 750g

3.5kg damsons
1 litre water
preserving sugar

1 Wash the damsons, put them into a large deep saucepan and cover with the water. Bring to a boil on the Boiling Plate, then move to the Simmering Oven for 1–1½ hours until they are soft and the stones rise to the surface.

2 Sieve the damson mix and measure the pulp. To every 550ml of pulp, add 450g of preserving sugar. Put the damson pulp and sugar into a stainless steel saucepan and bring to the boil on the Boiling Plate. You may have to move it back and forth from the Boiling Plate to the Simmering Plate if the heat is too intense. Do not let it stick or burn! Stir constantly until the sugar has dissolved.

3 When the sugar has dissolved, move to the Boiling Plate and boil rapidly for about 4-5 minutes. Skim off any scum as it appears. Test for a set (see page 14) then spoon into the clean, shallow plastic tubs with lids. It should be thick and fudgy, not runny. Seal tightly and label.

Conventional Cooking:
Cook on the hob.

quince cheese

makes 500–700g

2kg quinces
1 litre water
preserving sugar

1 Wash and buff the quinces as there can be fuzz on them. Chop into pieces, put into a large, deep pan and cover with the water. Bring to a boil on the Boiling Plate, then move to the Simmering Oven for 1–2 hours, or until soft.

2 Sieve the quince mix and measure the pulp. To every 550ml of pulp, add 450g of preserving sugar.

3 Put the quince pulp and sugar into a stainless steel saucepan and bring to the boil on the Boiling Plate. You may have to move it back and forth from the Boiling Plate to the Simmering Plate if the heat is too intense. Stir the mix until it is thick and paste-like. Do not let it stick or burn!

4 When it is ready, lay some Bake-O-Glide into a tin or on a flat surface and pour the quince paste on to the Bake-O-Glide. Leave it to cool completely, then either cut into large blocks, wrap well and store in the fridge, or chop into little cubes to serve or cook with. Store it in plastic tubs or glass jars.

Conventional Cooking:
Cook on the hob.

winter

what's in season?

December

Fruit
Apples (stored)
Cape gooseberries (hot house)
Cranberries (imported)
Forced rhubarb
Grapes (hot house)
Oranges (imported)
Pears (stored)
Pineapple (imported)
Pomegranates

Vegetables
Alfalfa
Beetroot
Broccoli
Brussels sprouts
Cabbage (Savoy)
Carrots (stored)
Cauliflower
Celeriac
Celery
Chicory
Endive
Garlic (new and stored)
Jerusalem artichokes
Kale
Leeks
Marrows
Onions (new and stored)
Parsnips
Potatoes (main crop and stored, see note on page 179)
Pumpkins and squashes
Salsify
Shallots (new and stored)
Swedes
Tomatoes (hot house)
Turnips
Wild mushrooms
Winter greens
Winter lettuce (hot house/polytunnels)

Herbs
Rosemary
Sage
Thyme

Nuts
Chestnuts

Meat
Grouse
Guinea fowl
Hare
Mutton
Partridge
Pigeon
Pork
Quail
Rabbit
Snipe
Venison
Wild boar
Wild duck
Wild goose
Woodcock

Fish and seafood
Brown crab
Cod
Herring
Lobster
Mackerel
Mussels
Oysters
Prawns
Sardines
Sea bass
Squid
Wild brown trout
Wild salmon

Dairy
Cheese (Beaufort, Cheddar, Gouda, Stilton, Vacherin Mont d'Or)

January

Fruit
Apples (stored)
Cranberries (imported)
Forced rhubarb
Grapes (hot house)
Pears (stored)
Pineapple (imported)
Seville oranges (imported)

Vegetables
Broccoli
Brussels sprouts
Cabbage (Savoy and red)
Carrots (stored)
Cauliflower
Celeriac
Celery
Chicory
Endive
Garlic (new and stored)
Jerusalem artichokes
Kale
Leeks
Marrows
Onions (new and stored)
Parsnips
Potatoes (main crop and stored, see note on page 179)
Salsify
Shallots (new and stored)
Swedes
Tomatoes (hot house)
Turnips
Winter greens
Winter lettuce (hot house/polytunnels)

Nuts
Chestnuts

Meat
Grouse
Guinea fowl
Hare
Mutton
Partridge
Pigeon
Pork
Quail
Rabbit
Snipe
Venison
Wild boar
Wild duck
Wild goose
Woodcock

Fish and seafood
Brown crab
Cod
Oysters
Sardines
Wild brown trout
Wild salmon

Dairy
Cheese (Beaufort, Cheddar, Fontina, Gouda, Stilton, Taleggio, Vacherin Mont d'Or)

February

Fruit
Apples (stored)
Forced rhubarb
Pears (stored)

Vegetables
Alfalfa
Broccoli
Brussels sprouts
Cabbage (Savoy and red)
Carrots (stored)
Cauliflower
Celeriac
Celery
Chicory
Endive
Garlic (new and stored)
Jerusalem artichokes
Kale
Leeks
Onions (new and stored)
Parsnips
Potatoes (main crop and stored, see note on page 179)
Salsify
Shallots (new and stored)
Swedes
Tomatoes (hot house)
Turnips
Winter greens
Winter lettuce (hot house/polytunnels)

Meat
Guinea fowl
Hare
Pigeon
Pork
Quail
Rabbit

Fish and seafood
Brown Crab
Cod
Oysters

Dairy
Cheese (Beaufort, Cheddar, Fontina, Gouda, Stilton, Taleggio, Tête de Moine, Vacherin Mont d'Or)

winter recipes

Soups and Starters
St Vincent's Oxtail Soup
Roasted Winter Vegetable Soup
Split Pea and Ham Soup
Jerusalem Artichoke Soup
Potted Crab
Oven-roasted Onion Dip
Stuffed Dates

Main Courses/Meat
Calves' Liver and Bacon
Beef with Ginger and Wasabi
Steak with Béarnaise Sauce
Game Pie
Venison Burgers with Roquefort Cheese
Chorizo, Chicory and Chive Frittata
Chicken Milano
Chicken with Thyme, Rosemary and
    Pine Nuts
Choucroute Garni
Simple Casserole with Dumplings
Cobbler Topping for Casseroles
Goose Cassoulet
Somerset Cider Braised Pork Belly

Main Courses/Fish
Cod with Garlic Shrimps
Arbroath Smokies with Pernod and
    Crème Fraîche
Kedgeree

Main Courses/Vegetarian
Macaroni Cheese
Winter Pizza
Cavolo Nero with Tagliatelle, Garlic
    and Cream
Red Chard, Red Onion and Lancashire
    Cheese Tart

Accompaniments
Winter Salad
Broccoli with Lemon Zest and Garlic
Grilled Radicchio
Potatoes with Fennel and Gorgonzola
    Cheese
Braised Red Cabbage
Leeks Braised in Cream
Chicory with Walnuts and Lemon Dressing

Desserts and Baking
Orange Slices with Rosemary and Honey
Hazelnut and Chestnut Roulade
Nut Tart
Queen of Puddings
Oatmeal Cookies
Chocolate Marron Cake
Winter Warmer
Orange and Coconut Cake

Thank goodness we can buy oxtail again. It is a wonderful cut and quite delicious. As a guide, two oxtails will feed about four people. To prepare them, simply wash and dry them and cut into 3cm lengths. Trim off any excess fat. This soup is what the nuns made at my father's school and he loves it to this day!

st vincent's oxtail soup

serves 4–6

50–60g dripping

3 onions, peeled and chopped

2 tsp sugar

1 oxtail, jointed

50g flour

1 wine glass of fortified wine, such as Marsala or Madeira

425ml tomato purée

1 organic lemon, sliced

4 tbsp chopped fresh parsley

salt

TO SERVE:

2 tbsp finely chopped fresh parsley

zest of 1 organic lemon

1 garlic clove, peeled and very finely chopped or grated

6 hard-boiled eggs, shelled and cut into quarters

1 Melt the dripping in a large frying pan on the Simmering Plate. Fry the onions with the sugar until browned and charred, then transfer to a large stockpot. Add the oxtail to the frying pan and brown. Transfer the oxtail to the pot.

2 Add the flour to the frying pan and cook for a few minutes. Add the wine and tomato purée and stir to form a paste. Add to the oxtail in the stock pot and cover with approximately 1.4 litres of water, or enough to just cover the oxtails. Add the sliced lemons and the parsley, and season with salt.

3 Bring to the boil on the Boiling Plate, then move to the Simmering Oven and cook for 2 hours or until thick and delicious.

4 Mix the parsley, lemon zest and garlic together and put into a bowl. Pour the soup into warmed bowls, arrange the hard-boiled eggs on top of the soup and serve with the parsley and lemon mix scattered over.

Conventional Cooking:
Cook on the hob.

roasted winter vegetable soup

serves 6

6 baby carrots or small carrots cut into roughly the same size

3 potatoes, washed and cut into wedges – don't peel them

3 red onions, outside paper removed, cut through the root into quarters

½ a swede, peeled and cut into chunks

½ tbsp chopped fresh rosemary leaves

½ tbsp thyme leaves

2 garlic cloves in their skins

3–4 tbsp olive oil

salt and pepper

pinch of sugar

1.5 litres good chicken stock

1 Tip all the ingredients except the stock into a large bowl or plastic bag and toss really well so that everything is well coated in the oil.

2 Line a large roasting tin with Bake-O-Glide and tip in the vegetables. Slide the tin on to the first set of runners of the Roasting Oven and roast for 30 minutes. Transfer the tin to the floor of the Roasting Oven for another 10 minutes or until the vegetables are tender and slightly charred.

3 When the vegetables have been roasted, tip them into a large saucepan with the stock and bring to a simmer on the Simmering Plate. Blitz them in a food processor in batches. Check the seasoning and serve with croutons made from a stale loaf of brioche.

Conventional Cooking:
Pre-heat the oven to 200°C/400°F/gas 6 and roast the vegetables as above. Make the soup on the hob.

Note:
To make great soup you need great stock so it is worth making your own, or buy good organic stock.

All the old-fashioned cuts of meat are coming back into fashion. I think it is entirely due to people who are interested in food buying these cheaper cuts of meat from top-class butchers, and eating them in fab restaurants which are using them with great success.

split pea and ham soup

serves 6–8

350g split green peas

6 peppercorns

1.5kg smoked collar of bacon

3 stalks of celery

3 small carrots, peeled

1 bay leaf

1 large onion, peeled and studded with cloves

1 Rinse the peas in cold water. Wrap the peppercorns in a muslin bag (for easy removal later).

2 Put all the ingredients into a large stockpot that will fit into the Simmering Oven. Cover with cold water and bring up to a boil on the Boiling Plate. Cover and transfer to the Simmering Oven for 2½–3 hours.

3 Transfer the bacon to a plate and discard the celery, carrots, bay leaf, peppercorns and onion. The peas should be soft. Taste the liquid for seasoning – you probably won't need to add any salt.

4 Either use a hand-held blender or food processor to blend the peas so you have a smoothish soup. Reheat if necessary, check the seasoning and serve with croutons. Serve the bacon separately as a main course.

Conventional Cooking:
Cook on the hob.

Jerusalem artichokes are part of the sunflower family and are a tuber. They taste a bit like a cross between a radish and a parsnip. They are fabulous lightly sautéed in butter or eaten very thinly sliced with olive oil and lemon juice. Beware – they do give you wind!

jerusalem artichoke soup

serves 4–6

275g Jerusalem artichokes, peeled and cut into chunks

250g potatoes, peeled and cut into chunks

1 large parsnip, peeled and cut into chunks

salt and pepper

about 1.5 litres or more of good chicken stock, to cover

100ml cream

olive oil, to serve

1 Put everything but the cream and olive oil into a large saucepan and cover with the stock.

2 Bring to a boil on the Boiling Plate, then move to the Simmering Oven for about 45–60 minutes or until the vegetables are really soft.

3 Whiz the soup with a hand blender or food processor, pour it back into the saucepan and stir in the cream. Check the seasoning and serve with a slick of fruity olive oil.

Conventional Cooking:
Cook on the hob.

potted crab

serves 8

200g clarified butter (see page 118) made with unsalted butter, plus another 200g for sealing

blade of mace

good grating of nutmeg

pinch of cayenne pepper

good grating of lemon zest

salt and pepper

680g white crab meat, picked over

1 Put the butter, spices and lemon zest into a bowl and slowly melt at the back of the Aga. Leave to infuse for at least 1 hour or more. Remove any large bits of spice, such as the blade of mace.

2 Gently stir the crab into the spiced butter and divide the mix between eight ramekins, leaving room for the clarified butter seal.

3 Put the ramekins into a roasting tin and pour in enough boiling water to come halfway up the sides of the ramekins. Bring to the boil on the Boiling Plate, then transfer to the Simmering Oven for 25 minutes. Remove the ramekins and allow to cool.

4 Melt more clarified butter and pour over the top of each ramekin to seal. Refrigerate until ready to serve.

5 Remove from the fridge 20 minutes before you want to serve. Serve with hot Melba toast.

Conventional cooking
Pre-heat the oven to 160°C/325°F/gas 3 and cook as above.

potted crab

oven-roasted onion dip

serves 6–8

2 large onions, peeled and sliced
olive oil
½ tsp golden caster sugar
sea salt
pepper
unsalted butter
200g cream cheese
120ml sour cream
120ml mayonnaise
dash of Tabasco sauce

1 Put the onion slices into a bowl, pour over 1 tablespoon of olive oil and stir in the sugar, some salt and pepper.

2 Heat up a knob of the butter in a shallow baking tray in the Roasting Oven. When it has melted, spread the onion slices on the tray, slide the tray on to the third set of runners and roast the onions for about 20–30 minutes or until they are caramelised, giving them a stir after 10 minutes.

3 Remove the onions from the tray with a slotted spoon, leaving behind any excess oil. Leave to cool completely – this stage can be done in advance.

4 When you are ready to make the dip, you have a choice – either whiz everything up in a food processor and have a smoother dip, or beat the cream cheese, sour cream and mayonnaise well, then fold in the onions and the rest of the seasoning. Taste for salt and pepper and add more Tabasco if necessary. Serve with vegetable crisps, raw vegetables and good-quality potato crisps.

Conventional Cooking:
Fry the onions in a frying pan on the hob.

stuffed dates

serves 6

18 Medjool dates
18 slices of pancetta
Mozzarella cheese, cut into 18 chunks

1 Place a shallow baking tray in the Roasting oven to warm up.

2 Remove the stones from the dates and stuff each one with a piece of Mozzarella. Wrap each date with a slice of pancetta and place them on a baking tray lined with Bake-O-Glide.

3 Slide the tray on to the first set of runners in the Roasting Oven and cook for 3 minutes, then turn over and continue to cook for another 3 minutes or until the pancetta is cooked and the cheese has melted.

4 Serve three dates per person with some good bread and olive oil.

Conventional Cooking:
Pre-heat the grill so that it is hot and grill on both sides.

oven-roasted onion dip

calves' liver and bacon

serves 4

sunflower oil

4 slices back bacon

50g butter

1 onion, peeled and thinly sliced

splash of ketchup (see page 99)

2 tbsp flour

salt

16 x 225g slices of calves' liver (all the tubes, membrane and veins must be removed)

1 Pour about a tablespoon of oil into a heavy-bottomed frying pan and place the pan on the floor of the Roasting Oven. When it is very hot, remove the pan and fry the bacon on the Simmering Plate until it is crispy around the edges. Remove the bacon and set aside on a warmed plate.

2 Add a knob of butter to the fat and when it foams, add the onion slices and fry until soft on the floor of the Roasting Oven. Add a squeeze of ketchup and stir well. Spoon on to the plate with the bacon. Wipe out the pan and pour in fresh oil.

3 Spoon the flour on to a plate and season with salt. Dust the liver slices in the seasoned flour and add a knob of butter to the pan. Heat this until hot on the Boiling Plate, then fry the slices of calves' liver for a few minutes per side, depending on how thick they are. Divide the liver among four plates and top each piece with some onions and a slice of bacon.

Conventional Cooking:

Cook on the hob in a frying pan.

beef with ginger and wasabi

serves 4–6

2 tbsp groundnut oil

1kg good-quality cubed beef, such as flank

2 large onions, peeled and chopped

1 tbsp sugar

1 tbsp Thai curry paste or Indian curry powder

6cm freshly grated ginger, or 2 tsp minced ginger

1 tbsp potato flour

700ml beef stock

50ml Worcestershire sauce

salt and pepper

1 tsp wasabi, or 3 tbsp freshly grated horseradish or made-up horseradish sauce

100ml crème fraîche

1 Heat the groundnut oil in a large heavy-bottomed pan on the Simmering Plate. Brown the meat pieces in batches and remove them to a plate.

2 Add the onions and sugar to the pan and place on the floor of the Roasting Oven. Cook until they are charred at the edges and starting to colour.

3 Move the pan to the Boiling Plate and stir in the curry paste, ginger and flour. Scrape up all the sticky bits on the bottom, then add about a wine glass full of stock to deglaze the pan.

4 Return the beef to the pan and stir well. Add the Worcestershire sauce and the remaining stock. If using wasabi, stir it in now. Stir and bring to the boil.

5 Put the grid shelf on the floor of the Roasting Oven, move the pan on to it and cook for 25 minutes, uncovered.

6 Cover the pan with a lid and move to the Simmering Oven, and continue to cook for another 1–2 hours. When you are ready to serve, stir in the crème fraîche. If using horseradish, stir it in now. Serve with rice.

Conventional Cooking:

Brown the meat in a frying pan on the hob. Pre-heat the oven to 190°C/375°F/gas 5 and cook for 1–1½ hours.

steak with béarnaise sauce

serves 4–5

850g very best quality beef flank steak

tasteless oil, such as grapeseed

salt

FOR THE BÉARNAISE SAUCE:

3 tbsp tarragon vinegar

1 shallot, peeled and finely chopped

4 black peppercorns, crushed

3 sprigs tarragon plus 1 tbsp chopped fresh tarragon leaves

2 sprigs chervil

3 large organic egg yolks

250g unsalted butter, cut into cubes

salt

1 Heat a ridged grill pan on the floor of the Roasting Oven for at least 10 minutes. (I sometimes put my pan in when I think of it, which can be an hour or so before I need it.)

2 Brush the flank steak with some oil and season it with salt. Remove the grill pan from the Roasting Oven and place on the Simmering Plate. Lay the steak in the pan and cook for 5 minutes, then flip over, season with more salt and cook for another 5 minutes. (This cut of beef is meant to be eaten either rare or medium.)

3 Rest for a few minutes on a warmed platter, then carve the meat in very thin slices diagonally across the grain.

4 Meanwhile, to make the sauce, put the vinegar, shallot, freshly crushed black pepper and herbs into a small saucepan on the Simmering Plate and simmer to reduce by half. Strain and add 1 tablespoon of water.

5 Place the egg yolks and the reduced vinegar mixture in a bowl over a pan of simmering water (do not let the bowl come into contact with the water) and whisk until the mix leaves a ribbon trail. Whisking constantly, drop in the cubes of butter one at a time – don't drop in the next cube until the previous one has been absorbed. This will take some time.

6 When all the butter is used up and you have a thick velvety sauce, check the seasoning and add the chopped tarragon. Serve the steak with the sauce, accompanied by bread and salad.

Conventional Cooking:
Make the sauce on the hob and cook the steak in a ridged grill pan heated up on the hob or on a barbecue.

Note:
For this recipe I use flank steak. This cut is extremely good and tender but must either be cooked for a short amount of time (as in this recipe) or a very long time.

It is best to make this pie a couple of days in advance to let the flavours develop. When game is not in season, replace it with pork. The chicken stock needs to be home made from a chicken carcass and reduced. It mustn't be too thin – aim for a loose jelly consistency. You can either make this pie in a traditional raised pie mould (as shown in the photograph) or use a 20.5cm round cake tin with a removable base and deep sides.

game pie

serves 6

FOR THE PASTRY:

450g plain flour

1 tsp salt

225g butter

2 large egg yolks

70–85ml ice cold water

FOR THE PIE FILLING:

sunflower oil

knob of butter

250g pheasant breasts, cut into chunks

200g lean veal, cubed

100g pigeon or chicken, cubed

85g pancetta, cubed

2–3 tbsp brandy, for deglazing

85g pork back fat, cubed

fresh thyme

salt and pepper

1 egg, beaten

500–600ml good home-made chicken stock

1 First make the pastry. Sift the flour and salt into a food processor bowl. Add the butter and pulse for a few seconds so the butter is rubbed into the flour, then add the yolks. Slowly add the water a little at a time (you may not need all of it) until it forms a dough. Wrap in cling film and refrigerate overnight.

2 Heat up about a tablespoon of oil and the butter in a large pan. Brown all the meat, including the pancetta, a batch at a time so they truly brown (don't overload the pan). Move the browned meat to a plate and deglaze the pan with the brandy, scraping up the caramelised bits. Set aside.

3 Roll the pastry out into a circle about 3cm thick. Grease a deep 20.5cm round cake tin with a removable base or a game pie mould. Cut a triangular 'slice' out of the pastry and set aside. Cone the rest of the pastry and fit it into the tin, letting the pastry overhang the sides. Press it well into the sides.

4 Spoon in the browned meat and pork fat, sprinkle over the thyme leaves and season with salt and pepper. Pour in any juices from the deglazed pan.

5 Roll out the triangle to make a lid. Cover the meat with the lid and fold in the overhanging pastry to meet the lid top so the filling is sealed in. Brush the top with beaten egg and make a generous-sized hole in the centre to allow steam to escape, and to fill with the stock after it has been cooked.

6 Bake the pie on the grid shelf on the floor of the Roasting Oven with the Cold Plain Shelf above for 15–20 minutes until the crust is set and starts to colour. For 4-oven Aga owners, bake in the Baking Oven for 20–25 minutes.

7 Move to the Simmering Oven for 1½–2 hours or until the meat is cooked (check by using a meat thermometer). If it colours too quickly, cover with foil.

8 Remove the pie from the oven and carefully pour the stock in through the hole in the pastry lid. (You may not need all the stock.)

9 Cool the pie completely before turning it out of the mould or tin.

Conventional Cooking:

Pre-heat the oven to 190°C/375°F/gas 5 and bake the pie for 25–30 minutes until the crust is set and starts to colour. Reduce the temperature to 180°C/350°F/gas 4 and cook the pie for a further 1–1½ hours or until the meat is cooked. You can check by using a meat thermometer. If the pie browns too quickly, cover the top with foil. Cool the pie completely before turning it out.

venison burgers with roquefort cheese

makes 4 medium-sized burgers or 6 smaller ones

olive oil

1 onion, peeled and finely chopped

500g lean venison

120g pork fat

fresh sage

1 tbsp tomato ketchup (see page 99)

1 tbsp Worcestershire sauce

salt and pepper

100g Roquefort cheese

burger buns, relish, pickles and crisps, to serve

1 Heat up some oil in a frying pan on the floor of the Roasting Oven and fry the onions until they are translucent.

2 Using a food processor, mince up the venison, pork fat, 6–7 sage leaves, ketchup, Worcestershire sauce, cooked onions, salt and pepper.

3 Put the frying pan back on the floor of the Roasting Oven to heat up again.

4 Shape the mince into flat burgers. Add a little more oil to the frying pan and fry the burgers on the floor of the Roasting Oven or on the Boiling or Simmering Plate, for about 2–3 minutes each side. They need to be cooked all the way through and a little charred on the outside.

5 Slice the cheese and top each burger with it and leave in the pan while you tend to the buns.

6 Split and toast the burger buns using the Aga toaster. Put a base of a bun on each plate and place a burger on one half of the bun and top with the other half of the bun. Serve with a good relish, pickles and crisps.

Conventional Cooking:
Cook on the hob.

Note:
Venison is a wonderful meat to eat as it so lean. Treat it as you would beef.

Chicories are closely related to dandelions and lettuce. The lovely fresh bitter taste is wonderful for salads, especially those that include nuts and fruit. Look for brightly coloured outer leaves, do not buy any with brown or wilted leaves.

chorizo, chicory and chive frittata

serves 4

olive oil

1 chorizo sausage, about 60–70g, sliced

2 small chicory heads or 1 medium-sized one

6–7 organic eggs

salt and pepper

1 bunch of chives

butter

100g mascarpone cheese

peel and juice of 1 organic lemon

Parmesan cheese, grated, to serve

1 Put a little oil in a heavy-based frying pan and fry the chorizo slices on the Boiling or Simmering Plate so they are crispy. Drain and set aside. Slice the chicory into wedges and fry them in the oil, drain, then wipe out the pan.

2 Lightly beat the eggs and season with a little salt and pepper. Chop up the chives and add to the eggs.

3 Heat up a tablespoon of oil and a knob of butter in the pan until melted, then pour in the egg mixture. Spoon over the mascarpone cheese, chorizo and the chicory and put the pan on the third set of runners in the Roasting Oven for 15–20 minutes or until it is lightly set. For 4-oven Aga owners, put the grid shelf on the third set of runners in the Baking Oven and bake for about 20 minutes or until lightly set.

4 Sprinkle over the Parmesan and put the frittata back into the oven for a few minutes. Remove from the oven and serve it either straight away or at room temperature. Cut in wedges and serve with a green salad and a drizzle of olive oil.

Conventional Cooking:
Start off the frittata on the hob, fry the chorizo and chicory in the pan. Drain them and wipe out the pan. Add more olive oil and butter, then add the eggs and swirl them around the pan to start to cook, then add the mascarpone cheese, chorizo and chicory, and leave on a low heat until it is lightly set. When it is ready, sprinkle over the Parmesan and put it in an oven pre-heated to 200°C/400°F/gas 6 for a few minutes.

chicken milano

serves 4

4 chicken breasts

4 tbsp flour

salt and pepper

1 large egg

2 sprigs rosemary leaves, stripped and chopped

60g Parmesan cheese, grated

breadcrumbs made from a stale loaf of focaccia bread

1 tbsp unsalted butter

olive oil

1 Flatten the chicken breasts between two pieces of cling film and beat with a rolling pin until thin.

2 Put the flour on to a flat plate and season with the salt and pepper. Break the egg on to another flattish plate and beat. Mix the rosemary and Parmesan with about two large handfuls (or more if you need it) of the breadcrumbs and put these on to a third plate.

3 Dip each chicken breast first into the flour, then the egg and then the breadcrumbs, really pressing them in.

4 Heat up the butter and a good glug of olive oil in a heavy-based frying pan on the Boiling Plate or the floor of the Roasting Oven until sizzling, then fry the chicken breasts for 2–3 minutes on each side. Keep warm in the Simmering Oven until they are all done. Serve the chicken with a green salad dressed with olive oil and a squeeze of lemon juice.

Conventional Cooking:

Fry in a frying pan on the hob.

Note:

This is traditionally made with veal, but chicken works just as well.

chicken with thyme, rosemary and pine nuts

serves 6

1.5–2kg organic chicken

olive oil

salt and pepper

300g basmati rice

750ml chicken stock

pinch of saffron

60g raisins, soaked in boiling water for 10 minutes

80g pine nuts, lightly toasted

4 sprigs thyme, leaves stripped and chopped

4 sprigs rosemary, leaves stripped and chopped

1 Put the chicken into a roasting tin and rub the olive oil generously into the bird. Season well with salt and pepper. Roast in the Roasting Oven for about 1 hour or until the birds are cooked and have a crispy skin.

2 Meanwhile, cook the rice in the stock and the saffron in a large pan. Bring up to the boil on the Boiling Plate, then cover with a lid and transfer to the floor of the Simmering Oven for 18–20 minutes.

3 When the chicken is ready, remove from the roasting tin (do not clean the tin), take all the meat off the bones and chop up the crispy skin. Put the roasting tin on the Simmering Plate and add the herbs, chicken, rice, drained raisins and pine nuts to the roasting tin and mix them together, letting the rice soak up all the pan juices. Check the seasoning and serve.

Conventional Cooking:

Pre-heat the oven to 180°C/350°F/gas 4 and roast for about 1 hour or until the chicken is cooked and has a crispy skin. Cook the rice on the hob.

choucroute garni

serves 10–12

2.2kg sauerkraut, drained

20 whole black peppercorns

1½ tsp coriander seeds

4 cloves

15 juniper berries

7 sprigs of flat-leaf parsley

4 sprigs fresh thyme

60g goose fat

4 medium onions, peeled and sliced

350ml dry white wine

500ml chicken stock

750g smoked belly pork

750g unsmoked belly pork

2 ham hocks

750g smoked gammon

3 carrots, peeled

3 garlic cloves, peeled and crushed

salt

10 small red potatoes, peeled

4 veal sausages

4 smoked sausages

4 Alsace sausages

1 Rinse the sauerkraut in a colander with warm water and drain. Make a bouquet garni with the peppercorns, coriander seeds, cloves, juniper berries, parsley and thyme. Wrap in muslin and secure with kitchen twine.

2 Melt the goose fat in a very large casserole dish on the Simmering Plate. Add the sliced onions and cook until they are translucent but not brown. Add the wine and chicken stock to the pot and stir well.

3 Next add both of the pork bellies, ham hocks, gammon, carrots, garlic, salt and bouquet garni. Lay the drained sauerkraut on top, then add enough cold water so that it comes to just below the sauerkraut. Cover and bring the liquid to the boil on the Boiling Plate. Transfer the pot to the Simmering Oven and cook at a simmer for 1½–2 hours.

4 Add the potatoes and cook for about 20 minutes or until tender. Finally add the sausages to the casserole and cook for about 10 minutes or until they are heated through.

5 To serve, remove the bouquet garni and discard. Transfer the meats to a large, warmed dish. Drain the sauerkraut and place in the middle of a serving platter. Slice the pork belly and gammon, and then arrange the meat and vegetables on and around the sauerkraut. Serve with lots of good beer, crusty bread and a selection of grainy mustards.

Conventional Cooking:
Make it on the hob, and use a low heat to simmer it for 1–1½ hours.

You can change the meat in this basic recipe to suit the season. The method for making a casserole is exactly the same and the Aga really comes into its own with this type of recipe!

simple casserole with dumplings

serves 6

65g flour

1.7kg meat – chuck steak, chicken pieces, pork, cut into 4cm cubes

100ml cooking olive oil

150g pancetta cubes or chopped bacon

8 shallots, peeled and quartered

2 garlic cloves, peeled and crushed

450ml wine, to suit meat – red for beef and white for chicken or pork

600ml good stock, to suit the meat

zest of ½ lemon (optional, but good with chicken)

salt and pepper

HERBS, TO SUIT THE MEAT:

pork: lemon thyme, flat leaf parsley, bay leaf

beef: thyme, flat leaf parsley, bay leaf

chicken: tarragon or rosemary or sage (not all three) and flat leaf parsley

1 Put the flour into a plastic bag and shake the meat pieces in it. You may have to do this in batches.

2 Heat up half the oil in a large casserole dish and brown the meat pieces in batches. Do not overcrowd the pan. You can do this on the Roasting Oven floor or on the Boiling Plate. Put the browned meat to one side.

3 Heat up the rest of the oil in the same casserole and add the pancetta or bacon and cook for a few minutes, then add the shallots and cook for 5 minutes or until they are soft. Add the garlic, but be careful not to burn it.

4 Pour the meat and the juices back into the casserole and add the wine, stock and herbs (and zest, if using) and season with salt and pepper. Bring to the boil on the Boiling Plate, then cover and transfer to the Roasting Oven for 20–30 minutes.

5 Remove from the Roasting Oven and stir. Move to the Simmering Oven and cook for a further 2½ hours. Calculate when you want to serve the casserole and then add the dumplings (see below) or cobbler topping (see right) 20 minutes before and move to the Roasting Oven and cook the topping there.

Conventional Cooking:
Brown the meat in a frying pan on the hob. Pre-heat the oven to 190°C/375°F/gas 5 and cook for 1½ hours or until the meat is tender.

dumplings

125g self-raising flour

50g shredded suet

2 tbsp chopped fresh flat leaf parsley or other herb to suit meat

salt and pepper

1 Sift the flour into a bowl and add the suet, herbs, salt and pepper. Mix together, then add about 3–4 tablespoons of cold water or more if needed, to form a soft dough.

2 Lightly flour your hands and pull off small pieces and roll them into a ball. Arrange them on top of the casserole and bake in the Roasting Oven 20 minutes before the casserole will be ready.

cobbler topping for casserole

500g self-raising flour, plus extra
salt
200g cold unsalted butter, cut
into pieces
2 tbsp chopped fresh herbs, to
suit meat
250ml buttermilk (see page 113,
and note below)

1 Sift the flour and some salt into a bowl, then rub in the butter so the mix resembles breadcrumbs. Stir in the herbs and pour in the buttermilk. Gently mix together so it forms a soft dough – do not overwork the dough or it will become tough. It should be slightly sticky.

2 Dust a surface with flour and flatten the dough with your hands. Using a cookie cutter or a knife, cut into rounds or squares. Arrange the cobbler rounds or squares on the top of the casserole and brush with milk.

3 Bake in the Roasting Oven for 10–15 minutes or until golden and puffed up.

Note:

The cobbler is cooked 15 minutes before the casserole is ready to serve. If you can't find buttermilk, use 250ml milk and sour with some lemon juice.

The goose is the king of the poultry yard. With its rich dark meat it is just what you want on cold dark winter nights. And, of course, there is nothing like goose fat for roasting potatoes.

goose cassoulet

serves 8

goose fat
3 large red onions, peeled and
chopped
1 head of garlic, peeled and
crushed
500g bacon lardons
1 goose, jointed
1kg flageolet beans, soaked
overnight in cold water
1 tbsp chopped fresh rosemary
1 tbsp thyme
salt and pepper
500g tin good quality tomatoes
30g tomato purée
900ml good chicken stock
5–6 slices country bread, at least
1 day old, made into crumbs
1 tbsp rosemary sprigs
olive oil

1 Heat up about 1 tablespoon of the goose fat in a large casserole or stockpot on the floor of the Roasting Oven and fry the onions until soft and brown, then add the crushed garlic and cook for just 1 minute. Using a slotted spoon, move the onions and garlic to a bowl.

2 Add another tablespoon of the fat to the casserole and fry the lardons until brown. Remove them to the onion mix. Add more fat if necessary to the casserole, then brown the goose in batches and put them to one side.

3 Drain the beans, then tip them into the casserole and add the chopped rosemary, thyme, salt, pepper, tomatoes, tomato purée and the onion mix, stirring well to coat every bean in the onions and garlic. Put the goose on top of the beans and pour in the stock to just cover – you may not need all of it.

4 Bring to the boil on the Boiling Plate, then put into the Roasting Oven for 25–30 minutes, and then move to the Simmering Oven for 2–3 hours.

5 Mix the breadcrumbs with the rosemary sprigs and scatter over the top of the cassoulet, drizzling over a little olive oil. Move to the Roasting Oven and cook for another 30 minutes until the top is crispy and golden.

Conventional Cooking:
Pre-heat the oven to 180°C/350°F/gas 4. Brown the meat in a frying pan on the hob. Bring to the boil for 8–10 minutes, then move to the oven for 2 hours.

If you want good pork, make sure it is well hung, a tasty breed – this is purely a matter of personal choice (I like Gloucestershire Old Spot and Saddleback) – and definitely from a kind farmer who knows his pigs!

somerset cider braised pork belly

serves 6

sunflower oil

1 onion, peeled and thickly sliced

2 bay leaves

6–8 juniper berries

1 apple, peeled, cored and sliced into rounds

2.5kg Somerset belly pork, cut into 6 slices

300ml chicken stock

300ml sweet Somerset cider, plus extra for deglazing

100ml double cream or crème fraîche

pepper

1 Heat about a tablespoon of the oil in a large shallow roasting tray on the floor of the Roasting Oven (my large traybake tin is perfect for this). Add the onions and fry until slightly charred around the edges. Drain off any excess oil and spread out the onions on the bottom of the tin.

2 Rip up the bay leaves, scatter over the onions and add the juniper berries and apple slices. Lay the belly pork slices over the onions and spices. Pour in the stock and cider so the meat is just covered – add a little more or a little less liquid if necessary.

3 Loosely cover the tin with foil and slide on to the third or fourth set of runners in the Roasting Oven. Braise for 20–30 minutes, then move to the Simmering Oven and continue to cook for another 1½–2 hours or until the meat is cooked and tender.

4 Remove from the oven, transfer the pork on to a warmed serving dish and keep warm. Finish off the sauce by putting the roasting tin on the Boiling Plate. Deglaze the pan with a little more cider if the liquid is almost all gone. Once that has bubbled for a few minutes, add the cream. Check the seasoning and pour over the pork. Serve with mashed potatoes.

Conventional Cooking:
Bring the casserole up to the boil over a medium hob heat, then transfer to an oven pre-heated to 180°C/350°F/gas 5 and cook for 2–2½ hours.

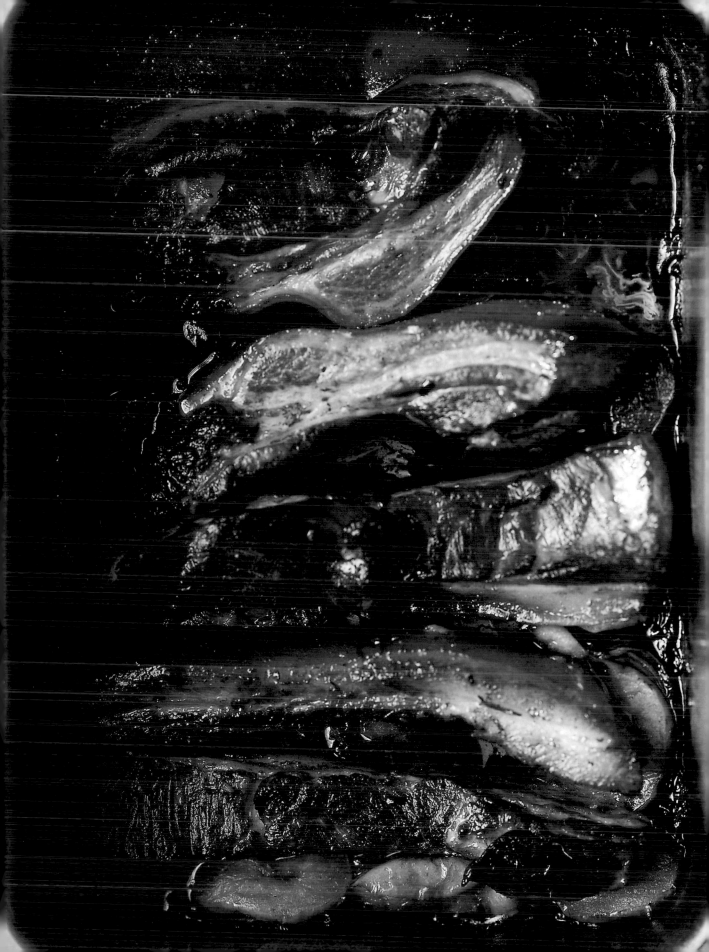

cod with garlic shrimps

serves 4

2 slices smoked bacon, cut into strips

100g unsalted butter

2 garlic cloves, peeled and crushed

salt

zest and juice of 1 organic lemon

1 tbsp chopped fresh parsley

100g shrimps or chopped prawns

4 x 180g cod fillets

1 Line a shallow baking tray with Bake-O-Glide. Slide the tray into the Roasting Oven to heat up.

2 Fry the bacon in a pan on the Simmering Plate or on the floor of the Roasting Oven until crispy. Drain and set aside.

3 Beat the butter in a bowl with the crushed garlic, very little salt if any, half of the lemon zest plus a squeeze of juice and the parsley. Mix in the shrimps or prawns and the bacon. Spread the top of the cod fillets with this mixture.

4 Remove the tray from the oven and place the cod fillets on the tray. Slide the tray back on to the floor of the Roasting Oven and cook for about 8–10 minutes or until the cod is cooked – this depends on how thick it is. Serve with the tray juices poured over and with buttery mashed potatoes.

Conventional Cooking:
Pre-heat the oven to 180°C/350°F/gas 4 and cook for 12–15 minutes as above.

arbroath smokies with pernod and crème fraîche

serves 8

30g butter

1 small onion, peeled and finely chopped

8 Arbroath Smokies, skinned, boned and flaked

2 tbsp Pernod

3 tbsp crème fraîche

top of a fennel bulb, chopped

salt and pepper

1 Put the butter and onion into a large frying pan and cook them on the floor of the Roasting Oven until they are soft but not coloured.

2 Transfer the frying pan to the Simmering Plate, add the Smokies and Pernod. Cook for a few minutes then add the crème fraîche and cook for 2 more minutes. Sprinkle in the fennel top, season, stir and spoon into eight shallow individual warmed dishes. Serve with rye bread and butter.

Conventional Cooking:
Place a frying pan with the butter in it over a medium heat and cook the onion until it is soft. Add the Smokies and Pernod and cook as above.

Cod is a wonderful fish but we all know about the shortages the seas are facing, so do also try haddock – it is a fine fish and one that deserves our utmost attention.

kedgeree

serves 6–8

300g cod, all bones removed

300g smoked haddock, all bones removed

500ml milk

500ml water

350g basmati rice

1 tbsp sunflower oil

1 onion, peeled and chopped

30g clarified butter (see page 118)

2 tsp Madras curry powder

1tbsp sultanas, plumped up with boiling water

2 tbsp chopped fresh flat leaf parsley, or watercress, plus extra for garnish

pepper

4 hard-boiled eggs, peeled and cut into quarters

1 Lay the fish in the large roasting tin and pour over the milk and water. Bring the liquid up to a simmer on the Simmering Plate. Take the tin off the heat and set aside to cool completely.

2 When it has cooled, remove the fish from the liquid. (Drain the milk, reserve and make a white sauce with it if you wish as sometimes kedgeree can be a bit dry.) Skin and flake the fish into large pieces.

3 Put the rice into a saucepan with a lid and add 625ml water. Bring the rice to the boil on the Boiling Plate, cover with the lid and transfer to the floor of the Simmering Oven for 20 minutes.

4 Put the sunflower oil into a frying pan and add the chopped onion. Place the frying pan on the floor of the Roasting Oven and fry the onions for 5–8 minutes, until they are soft and starting to char around the edges.

5 In the same frying pan, melt the clarified butter and add the curry powder and stir for a few minutes. Remove the onions from the pan with a slotted spoon and set aside. Remove the rice from the Simmering Oven and add the fish, onions, sultanas and parsley or watercress. Season to taste (you probably won't need to add salt) and mix gently with a fork to avoid breaking up the flakes of fish.

6 Transfer the kedgeree to a warmed serving dish and top with the hard-boiled eggs and sprinkle over a little more parsley or watercress.

Conventional Cooking:
Cook the fish, rice and onions on the hob.

Note:
This is a great dish for large numbers as it is easy to make and everyone enjoys it.

macaroni cheese

serves 6

500g macaroni
butter
700ml double cream
1 shallot, peeled and minced or grated on a microplane grater
500g mature Cheddar cheese
Worcestershire sauce
½ tsp English mustard powder
salt and pepper
200g Parmesan cheese
150g dried breadcrumbs, made from good bread

1 Cook the pasta in a large pan of plenty of salted water on the Boiling or Simmering Plate until it is tender but still has a bite to it. Drain and tip into a shallow buttered ovenproof dish.

2 Pour the cream into a saucepan, add the minced shallot and bring up to the boil on the Boiling Plate. Move to the Simmering Plate and add the Cheddar, a dash of Worcestershire sauce and the mustard powder. Stir until it has melted. Check the seasoning.

3 Pour the sauce over the pasta and stir well to make sure it is all coated. Sprinkle over the Parmesan, then the breadcrumbs. Put the dish on the third set of runners in the Roasting Oven and bake for 25–30 minutes or until the top is golden and bubbling.

Conventional Cooking:
Make the sauce on the hob. Pre-heat the oven to 180°C/350°F/gas 4 and cook for 30–35 minutes.

winter pizza

See page 132 for the basic pizza dough recipe and method. This is my list of suggested winter toppings:

Parmesan cheese
Mozzarella cheese
sun-dried tomatoes in olive oil
broccoli
lightly cooked chicory
mushrooms
dried oregano
chilli flakes
black olives

Cavolo nero is a member of the cabbage family and is used extensively in Italy, especially for Ribollita (see page 60). It has an almost sweet flavour and is a wonderful green/black colour. Prepare and use it like ordinary cabbage.

cavolo nero with tagliatelle, garlic and cream

serves 6

2kg cavolo nero
5 garlic cloves, peeled
250ml double cream
500g tagliatelle
salt and pepper
100g Parmesan cheese, grated
olive oil

1 Bring a large pan of water up to the boil on the Boiling Plate. Remove the stalks of the cavolo nero and blanch the leaves and two cloves of garlic in rapidly boiling salted water for 5–6 minutes. Remove the leaves and garlic with a slotted spoon and roughly chop with a knife. Set aside.

2 Pour the cream into a pan, add the remaining garlic cloves and bring up to a boil on the Boiling Plate. Watch the pan like a hawk so it doesn't overflow, then move to the Simmering Plate and reduce by half. This will take 10–12 minutes so, while you are reducing the cream, put a pan of water on for the pasta.

3 When the cream is ready, crush the garlic cloves with a fork into the cream (or discard the cloves if you don't want such a high intensity of garlic).

4 Cook the pasta in rapidly boiling salted water until it is done, then drain and pour into a large warmed bowl. Add the cooked cavolo nero and infused cream. Stir until the pasta is well coated in the cream. Check the seasoning, sprinkle over the Parmesan and add a slick of olive oil and some black pepper.

Conventional Cooking:
Cook the cavolo nero, the cream and the pasta on the hob.

Chard and beets derive from the same species, Beta Vulgaris. Chard should have fresh crisp leaves and good strong stalks. The larger leaves are sometimes the tenderest. Red chard is great tasting as well as being a delight to the eye. It is available from late spring right through to winter.

red chard, red onion and lancashire cheese tart

serves 4

olive oil

butter

2 red onions, peeled and thinly sliced

1 tbsp sugar

500g red chard, trimmed of the stalks and roughly cut up

salt and pepper

pinch of red chilli flakes

½ tsp thyme leaves

200g Lancashire cheese, crumbled or cubed

balsamic vinegar

FOR THE SAVOURY PASTRY:

175g plain flour

100g unsalted butter

1 egg

salt and pepper

1 Put all the pastry ingredients into a food processor and pulse until they come together to form a ball. Only add a drop of cold water if the mixture is crumbly. Wrap in cling film and rest in the fridge for at least 30 minutes.

2 Bring the pastry to room temperature and roll out to line a 20-cm tart tin. Line the pastry case with greaseproof paper and fill with ceramic baking beans. Bake on the floor of the Roasting Oven for 10–15 minutes or until golden brown. (The tart case can be baked in advance.)

3 Pour some olive oil into a frying pan, add a knob of butter and heat on the Boiling Plate. Move to the Simmering Plate, toss in the onions and sugar and cook until they are soft and slightly charred at the edges. Throw in the chard and cook until soft, then season with salt and pepper, thyme and chilli flakes.

4 Spoon the onion and chard mix into the tart case and crumble over the Lancashire cheese. Cook on the first set of runners in the Roasting Oven for 5–8 minutes until the cheese has melted and looks golden. Sprinkle over some balsamic vinegar and serve.

Conventional Cooking:
Pre-heat the oven to 180°C/350°F/gas 4 and bake for 15–18 minutes, then place under a hot grill to brown the cheesy top.

ACCOMPANIMENTS

winter salad

serves 8

200g chopped pecan nuts
1 fennel bulb
juice and zest of 1 lemon
1 Granny Smith apple
**240g seedless red grapes, cut
in half**
60g dried cherries
**100ml home-made mayonnaise
or really good store bought**
100ml crème fraîche
1 tsp honey
2 Belgian endives

1 Spread the pecan nuts on a baking tray and toast them in the Roasting Oven for about 5–8 minutes, keeping an eye on them to make sure they don't burn. Set aside to cool.

2 Slice the fennel very thinly using a mandolin or very sharp knife. Put it into a large bowl and squeeze over some lemon juice.

3 Cut the apple into thin wedges, leaving the skin on, and combine with the fennel, adding more lemon juice to prevent them browning. Add the grapes, dried cherries and nuts to the bowl.

4 Mix together the mayonnaise, crème fraîche and honey and gently fold into the fruit and nuts. Arrange the endive on the plates and spoon the salad on top. Scatter over a few extra nuts if desired.

Conventional Cooking:
Toast the pecan nuts under a hot grill.

broccoli with lemon zest and garlic

serves 4

100ml olive oil
1 garlic clove, peeled
1 organic lemon
salt
300g broccoli florets

1 Pour the olive oil into a small saucepan and crack the garlic clove with your palm or knife and drop into the oil. Peel the lemon, leaving as much of the white pith behind as possible and add that to the oil. Leave to infuse on the black enamel at the back of the Aga for a few hours.

2 Bring a saucepan of water up to the boil on the Boiling Plate, add salt and drop in the broccoli. Cook for about 2–3 minutes or until al dente.

3 Drain the broccoli into a bowl and squeeze over the juice of the lemon. Spoon over a couple of tablespoons of the infused oil, leaving the garlic and lemon peel behind. Toss and season with salt and pepper and serve.

Conventional Cooking:
Use a gentle heat to warm the oil and continue on the hob.

Note:
The remaining infused oil can be strained into a sterilised screw-top jar and stored in the refrigerator for up to 3 months.

grilled radicchio

serve 4–6

4 whole large radicchio
2 tbsp olive oil
salt and pepper
lemon wedges

1 Put a ridged grill pan on the floor of the Roasting Oven to heat up.

2 Split the radicchio heads in half, wash and spin dry. Put the radicchio halves in a shallow bowl and pour over the olive oil but don't drown them. Shake off the excess oil and season each half with salt and pepper.

3 Take the grill pan out of the oven and put it on to the Boiling Plate. Lay the radicchio halves in the searingly hot pan and grill for about 2 minutes on each side pressing down to flatten them. Serve them with wedges of lemon.

Conventional Cooking:
Pre-heat a grill pan on the hob and cook as above, or if you barbecue in the winter, use that!

Potatoes are classified according to when they are harvested – Main Crop potatoes are September to May; First Earlies (very new) are May to July; Second Earlies (new) are August to March. King Edwards, Maris Piper and Desiree are good all-rounder main crop potatoes. If you are into making your own crisps, Record is a good variety (any root vegetable can easily be made into crisps so do experiment). When buying potatoes avoid ones with green patches on them as this indicates light exposure which means toxins. Buy new potatoes in small quantities as they don't keep as well as main crop potatoes.

potatoes with fennel and gorgonzola cheese

serves 6

600g potatoes, peeled and chopped into chunks

3 large fennel bulbs, cut into quarters

5 garlic cloves, peeled

1 lemon

salt

300ml double cream

50g Parmesan cheese, grated

125g Gorgonzola cheese, cubed

85g unsalted butter cut into cubes, plus extra for greasing

4 ciabata crispbreads, roughly crumbled

1 Put the potatoes, fennel and garlic cloves into a saucepan of water. Squeeze in the lemon juice, and add some salt to the water. Bring to the boil on the Boiling Plate and boil until the potatoes and fennel are tender.

2 Transfer the potatoes and fennel with a slotted spoon to a buttered ovenproof dish. Tip away most of the water, reserving 85ml of the cooking water in the saucepan with the garlic cloves. Add the cream to the cooking water, bring back to the boil and reduce until thick.

3 Mash the garlic with a potato masher or fork and add the cheeses to the cream. Pour this over the potatoes and top with the butter. Bake in the Roasting Oven for 20–25 minutes, until crispy and golden, then sprinkle over the breadcrumbs. (You can make this dish in advance and re-heat if you wish.)

Conventional Cooking:
Make on the hob and bake in an oven pre-heated to 200°C/400°F/gas 6.

braised red cabbage

serves 4

100g goose fat
500g red cabbage, thinly sliced
2 apples, peeled and grated
100g brown sugar
salt and pepper
250ml red wine
250ml port

1 Melt the fat in a large casserole dish on the Simmering Plate and add the cabbage. Soften the cabbage for 5–10 minutes on the Simmering Plate, then add the grated apple, brown sugar, salt and pepper.

2 Pour in the wine and port and bring to the boil on the Boiling Plate for about 2 minutes.

3 Transfer the casserole to the Simmering Oven and cook, uncovered, for 20–30 minutes. Check the cabbage, then cover with a lid and leave to braise for 1½–2 hours in the Simmering Oven or until it is soft, dark and delicious.

Conventional Cooking:
Braise the cabbage on the hob over a very low heat (you may need to use a heat diffuser) or in an oven pre-heated to 140°C/275°F/gas 1, but check it doesn't dry out.

leeks braised in cream

serves 4

butter
500g leeks, washed, trimmed and split in half
100g Parmesan cheese, plus more for garnish
200ml double cream
salt and pepper
2 hard-boiled eggs, peeled and chopped

1 Butter an ovenproof dish and lay the leeks in lengthways.

2 Stir the Parmesan into the cream, pour over the leeks and season with a little salt and pepper. Bake in the Roasting Oven for 20 minutes or until the leeks are soft and the cream is bubbling.

3 Scatter over the chopped eggs and top with more Parmesan. Return to the oven for another 5 minutes or until golden and the cheese is melted.

Conventional Cooking:
Pre-heat the oven to 200°C/400°F/gas 6 and cook as above.

chicory with walnuts and lemon dressing

serves 6

1 tbsp lemon juice
2 tbsp grapeseed oil
1 tbsp olive oil
salt and pepper
1 tsp caster sugar
6 chicory heads
60g walnut pieces
1 tsp icing sugar
zest of 1 lemon

1 Whisk the lemon juice, oils, salt, pepper and caster sugar in a bowl and set aside.

2 Put the chicory heads into a lightly oiled shallow gratin dish and pour over the dressing. Cover with foil and bake in the Roasting Oven on the third set of runners for 20 minutes or until the chicory is tender.

3 While the chicory is baking, toss the walnut pieces in the icing sugar and spread them out in a shallow tin lined with Bake-O-Glide. Slide it on to the first set of runners in the Roasting Oven and caramelise for 5 minutes, taking care not to burn them.

4 When the chicory is ready, remove with a slotted spoon to a warmed serving dish. Scatter over the walnut pieces and spoon over the dressing. Top with the lemon zest and serve.

Conventional Cooking:
Pre-heat the oven to 190°C/375°F/gas 5 and bake as above.

DESSERTS AND BAKING

orange slices with rosemary and honey

serves 4–6

75ml organic honey
5 tsp orange water
1 sprig rosemary
6–8 oranges

1 Put the honey and orange water into a small saucepan. Pick off the leaves of the rosemary and gently bruise them in a pestle and mortar, then add to the saucepan. Place the pan on the Simmering Plate and stir – do not let the sauce boil. Remove from the heat and leave to infuse for 10–15 minutes.
2 Slices both ends off the oranges. Stand the fruit on one end and, using a very sharp knife, slice away the skin so that you take the pith and skin only, leaving as much flesh as possible. Slice the skinned oranges into thin pinwheels and remove any pips.
3 Arrange overlapping slices on a large platter. Pour over the honey and orange infusion. Serve with crème fraîche or on its own with plain biscuits.

Conventional Cooking:
Make the infused syrup on a low heat on the hob.

hazelnut and chestnut roulade

serves 4–6

4 eggs, separated
50g golden caster sugar
½ tsp baking powder
2 tbsp plain flour
50g ground hazelnuts

FOR THE FILLING:
350g tin unsweetened chestnut purée
80g icing sugar, plus more for dusting
1 tbsp brandy
150ml double cream, whipped
80g dark chocolate, grated
cocoa powder, for dusting

1 Line a small shallow baking tray with Bake-O-Glide and set aside.
2 Whisk the egg yolks and all but 1 tablespoon of the caster sugar together in a bowl.
3 In another bowl, whisk the egg whites to the soft peak stage, then add the reserved tablespoon of caster sugar. Sift the baking powder and flour in. Fold in the hazelnuts then fold in the yolks.
4 Pour the meringue on to the Bake-O-Glide and spread into the shape of the tray. Slide the tray on to the third set of runners in the Simmering Oven (for 4-oven Aga owners, use the middle runners) and bake for 30–40 minutes. Remove from the oven, cover with a clean damp tea towel and leave to cool completely. If you leave it to cool in the fridge you will have a slightly softer meringue, if you leave it out it will be slightly crisper.
5 To make the filling, beat the puréed chestnuts with the icing sugar and brandy. Taste and adjust the sugar.
6 When you are ready to roll it, gently press the meringue with your hands. Spread the purée over the roulade, then the whipped cream and the grated chocolate. Roll up the roulade and dust with icing sugar and cocoa powder.

Conventional Cooking:
Pre-heat the oven to 180°C/350°F/gas 4 and bake for 10–15 minutes or until done.

nut tart

serves 8

FOR THE PASTRY:

340g plain flour

225g butter, cold and cubed

1 egg, from the fridge

30g caster sugar

FOR THE FILLING:

250g mixed nuts, such as almonds, macadamias, hazelnuts and pecans, chopped

45g unsalted butter

160g granulated sugar

240ml golden syrup

3 eggs

1 tsp vanilla extract

85ml double cream

1 Put all the pastry ingredients into a food processor and pulse until they come together to form a ball. Only add a drop of cold water if it is crumbly. Wrap in cling film and rest in the fridge for at least 30 minutes. Bring to room temperature and roll out to line a 25cm tart tin.

2 Spread the nuts on a baking tray and toast them in the Roasting Oven for about 2–3 minutes, keeping an eye on them to make sure they don't burn. Set aside to cool.

3 Melt the butter in a bowl at the back of the Aga and set aside. In a medium-sized saucepan, combine the sugar and syrup and bring to the boil on the Simmering Plate. Simmer for 2 minutes, stirring constantly, then set aside to cool.

4 Beat the eggs, vanilla extract and cream in a large bowl, then stir in the melted butter and whisk in the golden syrup so that it is thoroughly combined. Add the nuts and set aside until completely cool.

5 Pour the filling into the chilled pastry. Place the pie on the floor of the Roasting Oven and bake for 20–25 minutes (if it browns too quickly, slide in the Cold Plain Shelf). Move the tart to a grid shelf on the floor of the Roasting Oven with the Cold Plain Shelf on the second set of runners. Continue to bake for a further 20–25 minutes or until the pie is cooked. For 4-oven Aga owners, transfer the tart to the Baking oven after the first 20 minutes of cooking time. Cool and serve at room temperature.

Conventional Cooking:

Pre-heat the oven to 200°C/400°F/gas 6. Bake the pie for 20 minutes, then lower the temperature to 180°C/350°F/gas 4 and continue to cook for about 20 minutes until the pastry is golden and the filling is set.

Notes:

You will have some pastry leftover from these quantities so freeze it either in a tart tin or rolled into a ball.

You will get about 25–30 minutes out of a Cold Plain Shelf, so you may need to cool the first one down halfway through the total cooking time or slide in another cold one.

queen of puddings

serves 4–6

225g golden caster sugar
zest of 1 lemon
100g white breadcrumbs
4 eggs (3 separated, 1 whole)
1 vanilla pod, split in half
600ml milk
4–5 tbsp raspberry or damson jam

1 Put 85g of the sugar into a bowl with the lemon zest and breadcrumbs.

2 Put one whole egg plus three egg yolks into another bowl.

3 Split the vanilla pod in half and scrape out the seeds. Tip the seeds into a saucepan, add the milk and bring just to the boil on the Simmering Plate. Stir the breadcrumb mix into the milk and whisk in the eggs. Allow to cool.

4 Pour the custard mix into an ovenproof dish and bake in the Simmering Oven for 1–1½ hours or until just set.

5 Spoon the jam into a saucepan and leave it at the back of the Aga to melt. When the pudding is ready, spread it evenly all over the pudding.

6 Whisk the remaining egg whites until soft peaks form, then whisk in the remaining sugar a tablespoon at a time. Spoon the meringue over the baked custard, sprinkle over a little more sugar and bake in the Roasting Oven for 8–10 minutes or until it is golden and set. Serve hot.

Conventional Cooking:
Heat the milk on the hob. Pre-heat the oven to 180°C/350°F/gas 4 and bake as above. When you are ready to put on the meringue topping, turn the heat up to 200°C/400°F/gas 6 and bake for 8–10 minutes or until golden and set.

oatmeal cookies

makes 15–20

240g unsalted butter
450g brown sugar
pinch of salt
½ tsp ground cinnamon
1 tsp baking powder
2 eggs
365g self-raising flour
1 tsp vanilla extract
160g oatmeal

1 Cream the butter and brown sugar together in a food processor with the paddle attachment.
2 Add the salt, cinnamon and baking powder to the flour.
3 Break one egg at a time into the butter and sugar mixture and mix, then add some flour until it is all incorporated. Add the second egg and the remaining flour, and mix. Add the vanilla extract. Mix in the oatmeal so that everything is evenly distributed.
4 Drop tablespoons of the mix 4cm apart on a baking tray and bake in the Roasting Oven on the fourth set of runners for 5–8 minutes. Cool on a wire rack. For 4-oven Aga owners, bake in the Baking Oven for 8–10 minutes.

Conventional Cooking:
Pre-heat the oven to 180°C/350°F/gas 4 and cook for 8–10 minutes.

Note:
If you are using a 2-oven Aga, try to bake the cookies when the ovens are a bit cooler. If you put the freshly cut raw cookies in the fridge for 30 minutes, it helps to stop them spreading. Raw cookie dough can also be wrapped in waxed paper and frozen or refrigerated, and slices can be cooked to order!

chocolate marron cake

serves 8

250g dark chocolate
250g unsalted butter
4 eggs, separated
milk (optional)
250g cooked chestnuts, finely chopped (vacuum-packed ones are fine)

1 Line a 25cm cake tin (loose bottomed or springform) with Bake-O-Glide.
2 Melt the chocolate and butter in a bowl at the back of the Aga or in the Simmering Oven. Mix the melted butter and chocolate mixture until you have a smooth batter. Add the yolks (you may have to add a little milk if it is too thick). Fold in the chestnut pieces.
3 Whisk the egg whites until stiff. Fold in a little of the whites into the purée to loosen, then gently fold in the remainder.
4 Pour into the prepared tin and bake in the Simmering Oven for about 1 hour – the cake should be a bit wobbly when it comes out. (If your Simmering Oven is fast, then check it before the hour is up, or if it is slow, it might take a lot longer.) Cool in the tin and serve with cream – it may collapse a bit but don't worry about that.

Conventional Cooking:
Pre-heat the oven to 170°C/340°F/gas 3½ and bake for 40–50 minutes or until it is just set but still has a bit of a wobble.

winter warmer

serves 4

2 tbsp double cream

**80g good quality milk chocolate
(or dark chocolate), grated**

**4 bakery-bought brioche buns
or mini round brioche**

1 Mix the cream and chocolate in a bowl.

2 Cut the tops off the brioche buns about one-third of the way down and hollow out the inside. Divide the chocolate mix between the brioches and replace the lids. Place the brioche in a roasting tin.

3 Slide the roasting tin on to the fourth set of runners in the Roasting Oven and slide in the Cold Plain Shelf on to the second set of runners. Bake for 10–12 minutes, or until the filling has melted and the brioche is crusty. For 4-oven Aga owners, bake in the Baking Oven for 10 minutes without the Cold Plain Shelf.

4 Serve straight away with fresh fruit for dipping into the centre.

Conventional Cooking:

Pre-heat the oven to 180°C/350°F/gas 4 and bake for 10–12 minutes, or until the filling has melted and the brioche is crusty.

Note:

This recipe is really just an assembly job! You can also use croissants.

orange and coconut cake

serves 8

butter, for greasing

2 oranges

6 eggs

185g caster sugar

250g desiccated coconut

1 tsp baking powder

1 Lightly grease a 20.5cm deep loose-bottomed cake tin.

2 Put the whole oranges into a saucepan of water, cover and bring to the boil on the Boiling Plate, then transfer to the Simmering Oven for 1 hour.

3 Drain the pan and whiz the oranges, skin and all, in a food processor until puréed. Remove any pips.

4 Whisk the eggs and sugar to a meringue-like consistency, then add the coconut, orange purée and baking powder and mix well. Pour into the prepared cake tin. Place on the grid shelf on the floor of the Roasting Oven with the Cold Plain shelf above, and cook for 20 minutes.

5 Transfer the cake to the Simmering Oven and continue cooking for 1–1½ hours or until it is cooked all the way through. For 4-oven Aga owners, bake in the Baking Oven for 50–60 minutes or until cooked. Cool and serve with Greek yoghurt.

Conventional Cooking:

Pre-heat the oven to 170°C/340°F/gas 3½ and cook for 40–50 minutes.

index

useful contacts

Amy Willcock
www.amywillcock.co.uk

The George Hotel
Quay Street
Yarmouth
Isle of Wight PO41 0PE
01983 760331
www.thegeorge.co.uk

Aga-Rayburn
08457 125207
ww.agarayburn.co.uk

Kitchenware

Rangeware by Amy Willcock
Mermaid
0121 554 2001
sales@mermaidcookware.com
My range of cookware

Chic Kit by Amy Willcock
01603 488019
sales@ictc.co.uk
My range of kitchen textiles

Aga-Rayburn
08457 125207
www.agalinks.com
www.agacookshop.co.uk
www.cookcraft.com

John Lewis
www.johnlewis.com
Kitchen equipment

Department Stores with Fab Food Halls

Fortnum and Mason
181 Piccadilly
London W1A 1ER
020 7734 8040
www.fortnumandmason.com

Selfridges
London, Manchester,
Birmingham
020 7629 1234
www.selfridges.co.uk

Harvey Nichols
London, Leeds, Birmingham,
Edinburgh, Manchester
020 7235 5000
www.harveynichols.com

Great Delis

Ceci Paolo
21 High Street
Ledbury
Herefordshire HR8 IDS
01531 632976
www.cecipaolo.com

Clarke's
124 Kensington Church
Street
London W8 4BH
020 7221 9225
(A great restaurant too)

Daylesford Organic Farm Shop
Moreton-in-Marsh
Gloucestershire GL56 0YG
01608 731700

La Fromagerie
2–4 Moxon Street
London W1 4EW
020 7935 0341

Villandry
170 Great Portland Street
London W1W 5QD
020 7631 3131

Organic Mail Order Suppliers

Swaddles Green Farm
Hare Lane
Buckland St Mary
Chard
Somerset TA20 3JR
0845 456 1768
www.swaddles.co.uk
Fresh organic meat by mail order

Jekka McVicar
Jekka's Herb Farm
Rose Cottage
Shellards Lane
Alveston
Bristol BS35 3SY
01454 418878
www.jekkasherbfarm.com
Fresh organic herbs by mail order

The Organic Gardening Catalogue
Riverdene Business Park
Molesey Road
Hersham
Surrey KT12 4RG
01932 253666
www.organiccatalog.com
Organic seeds and plants

Cookery Schools

Eggleston Hall
Eggleston
Barnard Castle
Co Durham DL12 0AG
01833 650 553
www.egglestonhall.co.uk

Padstow Seafood School
01841 533 466
www.rickstein.com
seafoodschool@rickstein.com

Leith's School of Food and Wine
21 St Alban's Grove
London W8 5BP
020 7229 0177
www.leiths.com

La Petite Cuisine
Lyn Hall
21 Queen's Gate Terrace
London SW7 5PR
Tel 020 7584 6841
Fax 020 7225 0169

Useful Associations

The Soil Association
Bristol House
40-56 Victoria Street
Bristol BS1 6BY
0117 929 0661
www.soilassociation.org

National Association of Farmers' Markets
c/o Farm Retail Association
PO Box 575
Southampton
Hampshire SO15 7BX
0845 230 2150
www.farmersmarkets.net

Bake-O-Glide
01706 224790
www.bakeoglide.co.uk

T N Cook
Close House Farm
Offley Road
Skipton
Yorkshire BD23 6DR
01756 792491
www.tncook.com
Kitchenware supplier

author's acknowledgements

I am hugely indebted to all the team for making this book so fabulous! Massive thanks to Gillian Haslam, Christine Wood and Tessa Evelegh – they have been there from the start and have been counsel as well as editor, designer and stylist; Grace Cheetham, Carey Smith, Stina Smemo, Helen Hutton and the Ebury team; the brilliant Sarah Wooldridge and Lucy Hutton at IMG; my chief recipe tester Anthony Audette; Kevin Mangeolles and all at The George Hotel; Peter Williams and Jason Lowe for great pics; Catherine for keeping everything running smoothly; and last but not least Jeremy, who always has a sense of humour whatever the weather! Thank you!